WEST COUNTRY LARDER

Traditional Recipes from

DEVON, CORNWALL
SOMERSET & DORSET

Compiled by Alison Ainsworth

Peninsula
Press

Published by Peninsula Press
P.O. Box 31
Newton Abbot
Devon TQ12 5XH

Editorial, Design and Production:
A&B Creative Services
Kingskerswell
Devon TQ12 5EZ
Tel: 0803 873599

Sales and Distribution:
Town & Country Books
Kingskerswell
Devon TQ12 5AZ
Tel: 0803 875875

Printed in England by Penwell Ltd, Callington, Cornwall.

ISBN 1 872640 04 4

WEST COUNTRY LARDER

❧ *Contents* ❧

INTRODUCTION

West Country Larder brings together a collection of traditional recipes, from simple homely dishes such as Easy Peasy Soup to the more sophisticated Mussels with Saffron. The cookery to be found in this part of Britain is as varied as the landscape itself, and recipes have been handed down through the generations, making full use of the wide variety of fresh ingredients available. Fish and seafood are plentiful: mackerel, haddock, red mullet, crab and mussels, to name but a few, and of course pilchards, without which there would have been no Starry-gazey Pie in Cornwall!

There is too, an abundance of the freshest fruit and vegetables, including leeks, carrots, celery, watercress, strawberries, pears, plums and apples. The apple must surely be one of the most versatile fruits, whether served as a sharp accompaniment to pork, made into puddings such as Apple Frumenty topped with plenty of thick clotted cream, or pressed into sparkling cider to wash down a Cornish Pasty.

Not all of the recipes are intended to be used; some are mentioned for their curiousity value, and include such items as Lamb's Tail Pie and Samphire Hash.

From the richness of Somerset Pork with Cider Cream Sauce to the comforting simplicity of Apple Dumplings, there will be something here to tempt every palate, and to give a glimpse of food served in years gone by.

WEST COUNTRY LARDER

Traditional Recipes from

DEVON

Compiled by Alison Ainsworth

*Peninsula
Press*

Published by Peninsula Press
P.O. Box 31
Newton Abbot
Devon TQ12 5XH

Editorial, Design and Production:
A&B Creative Services
Kingskerswell
Devon TQ12 5EZ
Tel: 0803 873599

Sales and Distribution:
Town & Country Books
Kingskerswell
Devon TQ12 5AZ
Tel: 0803 875875

Printed in England by Penwell Ltd, Callington, Cornwall.

The publishers would like to thank the many people of Devon who
have contributed to this book.

ISBN 1 872640 00 1

WEST COUNTRY LARDER
· DEVON ·

✍ *Contents* ✍

INTRODUCTION

Good food in Devon does not consist solely of cream teas, although clotted cream must surely be one of the county's most delectable products. In addition to dairy produce, the warmth of the Gulf Stream and the rich red fertile soil make ideal conditions in which to raise lambs, pigs and beef cattle, and by tradition no farm would have been complete without numerous chickens, ducks and geese free-ranging around the farmyard. The seas around Devon also provide an abundant harvest, and a wide variety of fish and seafood forms the basis of many local dishes.

The apple plays an important part in a county where orchards yield heavy crops for eating, cooking and of course for cider making. The glut of fruit in late summer and early autumn has stretched the ingenuity of cooks for centuries, ensuring that nothing is ever wasted. Cider Chicken is just one of many mouth-watering recipes which make full use of fresh local produce, including apples, cider and even clotted cream!

Fish & Seafood

Devonshire Crab Soup

Buttered Crab

Pilchards

Mackerel with Gooseberry Sauce

Smoked Mackerel

Smoked Mackerel Pâté

Soused Herrings

DEVONSHIRE CRAB SOUP

Crabs are still caught in large quantities in the sea around the West Country and Devonshire crabs are particularly good. Larger than most, their rich meat makes a delicious meal. This soup uses a medium-sized crab. If fresh crab is not available, frozen crabmeat can be used instead.

Ingredients
Serves 4 to 6

The cooked meat of one medium crab, or
8oz (225g) thawed frozen crabmeat
1 small onion
1 stick of celery
3oz (75g) long grain rice
1 pint (570ml) full cream milk
1 pint (570ml) fish or chicken stock
1/4 pint (150ml) double cream
2 tablespoons sherry
1-2 teaspoons anchovy essence
1/2oz (10g) butter
A good pinch of cayenne pepper
Salt and pepper

Method
Peel the onion and trim the celery, then chop both very finely. Melt the butter in a heavy-based saucepan and cook the onion and celery over a very low heat, until the onion becomes soft and transparent. Add the rice and milk, bring to the boil and simmer gently for about 15-20 minutes until the rice is cooked. Strain off and keep any excess milk.

Reserve about two tablespoons of the crabmeat, preferably from the claws, then either liquidise the remainder in a food processor, together with the vegetables and rice, or pass it through a fine sieve. Now return the puréed mixture to a clean saucepan and add the reserved milk and stock.

Season with salt and pepper, bring to the boil and simmer for 10 minutes. Add the cayenne pepper and anchovy essence, then stir in the sherry and cream. If the soup seems too thick you can add more milk. Heat through without boiling and serve at once, garnished with the reserved crabmeat.

BUTTERED CRAB

Ingredients
Serves 4 to 6

2 large crabs, or
1lb (450g) thawed frozen crabmeat
2 anchovy fillets
1/2 pint (275ml) white wine
1 cup white breadcrumbs
3 tablespoons softened butter
A pinch of freshly grated nutmeg
Salt and pepper

Method
Mash the anchovy fillets with the wine, mix with the breadcrumbs and season with nutmeg, salt and pepper. Bring gently to the boil and simmer for 5 minutes. Mix the flaked crabmeat with the softened butter and add to the wine and breadcrumb mixture. Cook for a further 5 minutes then serve with hot buttered toast.

PILCHARDS

Pilchards once provided the fishermen of Devon and Cornwall with their biggest catches. During his tour of England and Wales in the 1720's, Daniel Defoe was with a friend in a boat at the mouth of the River Dart. He saw *"some small fish to skip, and play upon the surface of the water, upon which I asked my friend what fish they were; immediately one of the rowers of seamen starts up in the boat, and throwing his arms abroad, as if he had been bewitch'd, cryes out as loud as he could baul, 'A scool a scool!' The word was taken to the shore as hastily as it would have been on land if he had cry'd fire."*

Later, Defoe and his friends ate a pilchard dinner which cost three farthings altogether. The fresh pilchards were simply grilled, and sprinkled with salt and pepper.

MACKEREL WITH GOOSEBERRY SAUCE

Mackerel and gooseberries both come into season at about the same time - May - and have been served together in this country since at least the seventeenth century. The tartness of the gooseberry offsets the oil-iness of the mackerel extremely well. Rhubarb is also mentioned in traditional recipes. Whichever is used, be careful not to add too much sugar, or the contrast of flavours will be lost.

Ingredients
Serves 6

6 mackerel, cleaned
Salt and pepper

For the sauce:
12oz (350g) gooseberries, topped and tailed
1oz (25g) butter
Sugar (to taste)
1/2 teaspoon ground ginger or freshly grated
nutmeg
1 egg, beaten

Method

Melt the butter in a saucepan and add the gooseberries. Cover closely and cook gently over a low heat. When the gooseberries are soft (after about fifteen minutes), put them through a sieve then return the fruit purée to a clean saucepan, add sugar to taste, and ginger or nutmeg.

Set the grill at its hottest. Lay the fish on the grill rack and season both the insides and outsides with salt and plenty of freshly ground black pepper. If the fish are quite thick - 1" (2.5cm) at the thickest part - grill at the highest heat for about 5 minutes on each side. Thinner fish will require less time. When you turn the fish over, start reheating the sauce. Once the fish are cooked, put them on a preheated serving dish. When the sauce has almost started to boil, remove from the heat and stir in the beaten egg. Heat through again, but do not allow to boil or it will curdle. Serve the sauce separately.

SMOKED MACKEREL

Mackerel provides one of the most abundant harvests from the sea around Devon, but it must be eaten very soon after being caught as it does not keep. In the nineteenth century it was the only fish that was permitted to be sold on the streets on a Sunday for the very reason that it would not be fit to eat if kept over the weekend. Mackerel smokeries were set up in Devon and Cornwall to extend the 'shelf life' of the fish.

Smoked mackerel makes a nourishing and fairly economical meal. One fillet served with a green salad and some crusty granary bread makes a delicious lunch or light supper dish. Try serving it with mayonnaise mixed with an equal quantity of gooseberry purée - a deliciously sharp accompaniment.

SMOKED MACKEREL PÂTÉ

Ingredients
Serves 8

2 medium smoked mackerel
4oz (110g) cottage cheese
1/4 pint (150ml) fresh or soured cream
Juice of half a lemon
Salt and black pepper
Nutmeg

Method
Skin and bone the mackerel, then flake the flesh into a food processor or liquidiser, together with the cottage cheese, cream and lemon juice. Blend until smooth, season with salt, pepper and grated nutmeg, and spoon into individual ramekins. Cover and chill before serving with wholemeal toast.

SOUSED HERRINGS

The fishermen who lived along the north coast of Devon during the eighteenth and nineteenth centuries caught plentiful supplies of cod and herring, indeed it is reported that in 1810 it took 400 horses to carry the catch of cod and herring up the steep shores that are typical of this part of the county.

As with mackerel, herring were often smoked, but another means of preserving was by sousing, or pickling them. In those days, the soused fish were sold from large earthenware pans, and taken home in the customer's own dish.

Ingredients
Serves 4

4 herrings (ask the fishmonger to fillet them for you)
1 small onion
1 bay leaf
1/4 pint (150ml) vinegar
1/4 pint (150ml) water
10 peppercorns
5 cloves
Pinch of salt

Roll up the fillets of fish and place in a baking dish with the sliced onion and the other ingredients. Bake in a moderate oven at 180°C (350°F), gas mark 4, for about an hour. Let it get completely cold, then add a little soft brown sugar. Cover, and keep refrigerated until required.

Meat & Poultry

Pot Roast of Beef

Beef Stew in Cider
with Parsley Dumplings

Pig Curing and Pork

To Cure Belly of Pork

Devon Pork Pie

Squab Pie

A Goodlie Pie

Cider Chicken

Lark Pie

Chicken Dumplings

POT ROAST OF BEEF

In years gone by, Devonians depended on peat to fuel their fires, and these were not suited to roasting meat. Instead, the meat was sometimes pot roasted in a 'baking oven'. This was a large, cast iron pot with a close-fitting lid and short handles. The meat and some dripping were put in the pot, the lid replaced, and the pot put in the hottest part of the fire. Hot ashes were raked up over the sides and top of the pot. The meat cooked beautifully in its own juices. Families who did not own a 'baking oven' could take their meat to the local baker to be cooked for the midday meal.

At the turn of the nineteenth centry a Devon ironfounder called George Bodley patented the very first cast iron closed top cooking range. This revolutionised the kitchens of the more prosperous families.

Ingredients
Serves 4 to 6

2½ - 3lb (1.1 - 1.4kg) fresh silverside or
topside of beef
2 large onions
8oz (225g) carrots
1 medium swede or turnip
1/2 pint (275ml) beef stock
1/4 pint (150ml) red wine
2oz (50g) butter
1 teaspoon fresh thyme, or 1/4 teaspoon
dried thyme
1 clove garlic
Salt and pepper

Method

Melt the butter in a pan and fry the beef on all sides until it is well browned. Remove the meat from the pan. Peel and quarter the onions, scrape and slice the carrots and peel and chop the swede or turnip. Soften the vegetables in the melted butter then put them into a large, deep casserole. The browned beef is then placed on top of the vegetables, seasoned with salt and pepper and sprinkled with thyme and crushed garlic. Pour in the stock and wine and cover with a lid of foil.

Cook in a preheated oven at 180°C (350°F), gas mark 4, for 1½ hours or until tender. Remove the lid for the last 20 minutes to brown the meat.

Serve the meat on a large serving plate surrounded by the vegetables. The gravy can be served as it is or thickened with a little cornflour if preferred.

BEEF STEW IN CIDER WITH PARSLEY DUMPLINGS

Parsley has always played an important part in Devonshire cuisine. It makes a particularly pleasing addition to dumplings, as does the cider in which the beef is cooked.

Ingredients for the dumplings
Serves 6

2oz (50g) self-raising flour
2oz (50g) fresh breadcrumbs
2 tablespoons shredded suet
2 teaspoons finely grated lemon rind
1 egg
1 tablespoon finely chopped parsley
Salt and pepper

Method

In a large bowl mix together the flour, breadcrumbs, suet, lemon rind, parsley and seasoning. Add the beaten egg and with lightly floured hands shape the mixture into small balls about the size of walnuts.

Ingredients for the stew
Serves 6

2lb (900g) shin of beef
8oz (225g) onions
8oz (225g) carrots
8oz (225g) turnips
2 sticks celery
1 pint (570ml) beef stock
1/2 pint (275ml) cider
1 ½oz (40g) well-seasoned flour
2oz (50g) beef dripping
Salt and freshly ground black pepper

Method

Cut the meat into 1" (2.5mm) cubes and toss in the seasoned flour. Heat the dripping in a large heavy-based pan or flameproof casserole, then soften the onions and brown the meat in it. Add stock, cider and seasoning and bring to the boil, removing any scum from the surface with a slotted spoon. Now add the carrots and turnips, peeled and diced, and the celery, cleaned and diced. Reduce the heat, cover the pot or casserole with a lid and simmer for about 2½ hours or until the meat is tender.

Place the dumplings on top of the stew for the last 20 minutes of cooking time.

PIG CURING AND PORK

"Have in a vessel 8 quarts of boiling water, add 7lbs bay salt, 2oz salt prunella and 1lb treacle and stir until all are dissolved. Place freshly cut hams in an earthenware standard, then, when this pickle is cold, pour it over them. After 6 weeks, take hams out, thoroughly dry them, put in muslin bags and store in malt dust, or wood ashes. Better still, if an open fireplace is available on which wood is regularly burnt, hang hams in the chimney for a fortnight before storing."

A Devonshire cure for bacon.

TO CURE BELLY OF PORK

"I have bought from the butcher belly of pork, and I have cured it as one does bacon, that is about 4lb at a time, rubbed it over with Demerara sugar first, and then with a coarse kitchen salt, and left it for about 4 or 5 days, turning and rubbing it with the liquid every day. Then I wash it and put it in the pan with 3 or 4 bay leaves, a tablespoonful of sugar and about 12 to 14 peppercorns. I boil it in wine for about 6 hours and then press it between two plates. When it is cold it is really delicious. One can eat skin and all."

From a Devon farmer's wife.

DEVON PORK PIE

"The squab pye, the herb pye, the leek and pork pye, on which clouted cream was profusely poured - the goose and the parsnip, and the fish and apple pye were frequent . . . . "

Richard Polwhele, Traditions and Recollections, 1816.

Ingredients
Serves 6

6 boned pork loin chops
3 medium onions or six medium leeks
6 cooking apples
1 pint (570ml) cider
8oz (225g) shortcrust pastry
2 tablespoons sugar
Pinch of freshly grated nutmeg
Pinch of allspice
Salt and pepper

Method
Trim the fat from the chops and cut in half if very large. Peel, core and slice the apples. Peel and slice the onions or leeks. Put three of the chops in a deep pie dish, followed by a layer of apples. Sprinkle with half of the sugar and spices. Now add a layer of onions, and season with salt and pepper. Repeat these layers, then pour over the cider.

Moisten the edges of the pie dish with water, roll out the pastry and fit it over the dish, pressing the edges down well. Brush the top with milk, make two small holes for the steam to escape, and put in a moderate oven 190°C (375°F) gas mark 5, for 15 minutes, then cover the pastry with foil, reduce the heat to 150°C (300°F) gas mark 2 and continue baking for a further 1¼ hours. It was traditional to pour over some warmed clotted cream, but this may make the dish too rich for present day tastes.

SQUAB PIE

Another very old recipe, young pigeons were the main ingredient of this dish. Nowadays, however, pigeons are not as cheap as they once were, and gradually mutton, then lamb, was used instead.

Ingredients
Serves 4

1lb (450g) neck of lamb chops
1lb (450g) cooking apples
2 medium onions
12oz (350g) shortcrust pastry
1/4 pint (150ml) cider or stock
1 level teaspoon cinnamon
1 rounded tablespoon sugar

Method
Peel, core and slice the apples and skin and slice the onions. Put half of the apples and onions in a pie dish and arrange the chops on top. Season well with salt, pepper and cinnamon. Cover with the remaining apple and onion. Roll out the pastry to fit the top of the pie dish. Flute the edges and use any leftover pastry to make leaves to decorate the top. Brush with milk and make two small holes for the steam to escape. Bake in the oven at 200°C (400°F) gas mark 6 for 30 minutes. Reduce the heat to 170°C (325°F) gas mark 3, cover with foil and cook for a further 40 minutes. As with the pork pie, it was fashionable to pour *'clouted'* - or clotted - cream over the pie before serving it.

A GOODLIE PIE

"Take small chickeyens . . . make of pastrie the best. Then lay the chickeyens side by side on the pastrie after filling their bellies full of bredcrumbs mixed with fresh butter, parsley, thyme, pepper and salt. Wrap pastrie over them, wetting and moulding the edges together. Bake in a Dutch oven before the fire, turning occasionally, till pastrie is golden, then serve in a deep oval dish, and hand round this Egg and Wine sauce, in a sauceboat along it: Mix 6 beaten egg yolks with white wine, vinegar, pepper, salt and ground cinnamon, sugar and rosewater to taste, and cook till sauce thickens."

From a 17th century recipe.

CIDER CHICKEN

This recipe combines several ingredients provided by Devon farms - chicken, apples, cider and clotted cream.

Ingredients
Serves 4

4 chicken pieces
1 medium onion
2 eating apples
1/2 pint (275ml) cider
1/4 pint (150ml) stock
1/4 pint (150ml) clotted cream
3oz (75g) butter
2oz (50g) flour
Salt and pepper

Method

Dust the chicken pieces with half the flour, seasoned, then fry them in 2oz (50g) of the butter until brown. Remove from the pan with a slotted spoon and place in a casserole. Peel, core and chop one of the apples and slice the onion. Fry these in the pan over a low heat until soft. Stir in the remaining flour and cook for 1 minute, gradually adding the cider and stock. Bring the mixture to the boil and pour over the chicken pieces. Cover the casserole and cook in a preheated oven at 180°C (350°F) gas mark 4 for about 45 minutes. Remove the chicken from the casserole, again using a slotted spoon. Keep the chicken warm and pour the liquid from the casserole into a saucepan. Reduce the liquid by boiling for 5-10 minutes. Slice the second apple and fry in the remaining butter. Add the cream to the sauce, but do not allow to boil again. Arrange the apple slices on top of the chicken and pour over the sauce.

LARK PIE

This 17th century recipe is not intended to be used, but is included purely for its curiosity value!

"Take as many larks as you please, season them with Pepper and Salt, put some forcemeat in the Bellies and balls of the same in the Pie with them, lay some very thin slices of Bacon upon the Larks if you like, if not put some Butter, put in a little thin Gravy when it comes out of the Oven give it a Shake; to have a fine Lark Pie add a few Palates - Lamb Stones or Sweet Breads, hard yolks of Eggs, Asparagus Tops, dry'd Mushrooms; make a Ragoo of all these things and when the Larks are bak'd open the Pie and throw it over the Larks, give it a shake, let it stand quarter of an Hour by the fire."

From a 17th century manuscript Receipt Book.

CHICKEN DUMPLINGS

Dumplings played an important part in the life of country folk, particularly before the introduction of the potato in the 16th century.

Ingredients
Serves 4

1 boiling fowl, with giblets
2 rashers bacon
8oz (225g) fresh white breadcrumbs
2oz (50g) grated cheddar cheese
1/4 pint (150ml) clotted cream
2 beaten eggs and 2 egg yolks
A sprig of parsley, finely chopped
Salt and pepper

Method

Put the chicken and giblets (except the liver) in a large saucepan, cover with cold water and bring to the boil. Simmer until tender. Fry the bacon and add the chicken liver when the bacon fat starts to run. Lift the cooked chicken out of the pot and allow to cool slightly, reserving the liquid, then remove the flesh from the bones. Put the chicken meat, the giblets, liver and bacon through a mincer or process for the shortest possible time in a food processor. Mix with the breadcrumbs and chopped parsley, and bind together with the two beaten eggs. Season.

Divide the mixture into four dumplings and put them in a large saucepan. Cover with 1 ½ pints (850ml) of the cooking liquid, bring to the boil and simmer for 15 minutes. Lift the dumplings out of the liquid with a slotted spoon and keep warm in an ovenproof dish. Beat together the egg yolks and cream. Stir in 1/2 pint (275ml) of the cooking liquid and heat gently, without boiling, until the mixture thickens. Pour the sauce over the dumplings and sprinkle with grated cheese. Brown under a preheated grill.

Cakes &
Puddings

Chudleighs

Gingerbread

Revel Buns

Lady Plymouth's Cake

Lady Plymouth's Apple Pudding

Whortleberry and Apple Pie

Apple Dumplings

Apple In and Out

To preserve Sweet Apples

Exeter Pudding

Clotted Cream

Devonshire Junket

CHUDLEIGHS

Probably better known as Devonshire Splits, but also called Rounds, Tuffs, Farthing and Ha'penny Buns, these are usually served warm, split open and filled with jam and clotted cream.

The traditional method used yeast as the raising agent. This recipe uses self-raising flour and takes far less time, but the results are just as delicious.

Ingredients
Makes 10

8oz (225g) self-raising flour
3oz (75g) margarine
2oz (50g) caster sugar
Milk
Pinch of salt

Method

Sift the flour and salt together and rub in the margarine until the mixture resembles fine breadcrumbs. Add the sugar and enough milk to mix to a fairly stiff dough. Turn onto a floured board and knead well. Roll out to about 1/2" (1cm) thick and cut into 2½" (6cm) rounds. Place on a greased baking tray and bake in a preheated oven at 400°C (200°F) gas mark 6 for about 15 minutes, or until well-risen. Allow to cool a little, then split and fill with home-made strawberry or raspberry jam and plenty of clotted cream.

GINGERBREAD

> *Tom Pearse, Tom Pearse, lend me thy grey mare,*
> *All along, down along, out along, lee.*
> *For I want to go to Widecombe Fair,*
> *Wi' Bill Brewer, Jan Stewer, Peter Gurney,*
> *Peter Davey, Dan'l Whiddon, Harry Hawk,*
> *Old Uncle Tom Cobbleigh and all,*
> *Old Uncle Tom Cobbleigh and all.*
>
> *Traditional*

Special sweetmeats, gingerbread and spiced ale were traditionally served at Widecombe Fair, probably the most famous of all the West Country fairs.

Ingredients
Makes about 12 portions

6oz (175g) plain flour
6oz (175g) brown sugar
6oz (175g) black treacle
5oz (150g) butter or margarine
1 teaspoon ground ginger
Pinch of bicarbonate of soda dissolved in
1 tablespoon of warm milk

Method
Beat together the sugar and slightly softened butter. Add the treacle and mix well until creamy. Sieve the flour and ginger and fold into the mixture. Add the dissolved bicarbonate of soda and milk and mix in well. With well-floured hands form the mixture into about 12 portions and place them well apart on a greased baking tray. Bake at 190°C (375°F) gas mark 5 for about 15 minutes, or until crisp.

REVEL BUNS

These were - and still are - made for village festivals, particularly those held to celebrate church anniversaries. In the old days the buns were placed on sycamore leaves before being baked.

Ingredients
Makes about 20-24

1 ½lb (700g) plain flour
1lb (450g) sugar
12oz (350g) clotted cream
8oz (225g) butter
6oz (175g) currants
1 egg
1oz (25g) yeast
1/4 pint (150ml) milk
1 teaspoon ground cinnamon
1/2 teaspoon saffron
Pinch of salt

Method

Rub the butter into the flour and add the sugar. Warm a little of the milk. Tie the saffron in a small square of muslin and leave it to infuse in the warmed milk. Warm the cream in a very low oven and mix the yeast and sugar with a little warm water.

Blend together the cream, flour, beaten egg and cinnamon. Remove the saffron from the muslin and add it to the mixture, together with the yeast, milk and currants. Cover and leave to rise in a warm place for 12 hours.

Form the mixture into small buns and place on a greased baking tray. Bake in a preheated oven at 190°C (375°F) gas mark 4 for about 30 minutes. Sprinkle with icing sugar when cool.

LADY PLYMOUTH'S CAKE

"Take 6lbs flour, 8lbs of currants, 1lb of sugar, some spice, 1lb of almmonds beaten, 1/2lb of cittron, 3lbs of butter, a quart of cream, 12 eggs, a quart of yest mix altogether let it rise an Hour bake it in a Hoop, Ice the Top."

From a 17th century manuscript Receipt Book.

LADY PLYMOUTH'S APPLE PUDDING

"Take 6 apples and coddle them, then take off the rind and core them, put them in a marble mortar with 5 eggs, leave out the whites of 2, a maple bisket grated, take the peel of an orange or lemon boil it soft beat it a little by itself, then put it into the mortar with 6oz of butter, sweeten it to your taste, beat it all together very well, put it in a dish with Puff Paste Top and Bottom, bake it an hour."

From a 17th century manuscript Receipt Book.

WHORTLEBERRY AND APPLE PIE

Whortleberries are also known as bilberries, blueberries or blaeberries. They are smaller than blackcurrants and not always easy to spot, so it takes quite a long time to pick enough for a pie. That is why it is best to add some cooking apples.

Ingredients

1 ½lb (700g) whortleberries
8oz (225g) cooking apples
6oz (175g) shortcrust pastry
4oz (110g) sugar
4 fl oz (110ml) water
1 egg white
Caster sugar

Method

Peel, core and slice the apples and put in a saucepan with the whortle-berries, sugar and water. Bring to the boil and simmer for 3 minutes. Transfer the fruit to a pie dish and allow to cool. Roll out the pastry and cut out a strip to cover the lip of the pie dish. Press the pastry strip onto the pie dish, dampen with water, and cover with the remaining pastry. Make 2 slits in the lid for the steam to escape. Brush the pie with the beaten white of egg and sprinkle with a little caster sugar.

Bake in the centre of an oven preheated to 200°C (400°F) gas mark 6 for 35-40 minutes until golden brown. Serve with clotted cream.

APPLE DUMPLINGS

Ingredients
Serves 4

4 large cooking apples
4 teaspoons mincemeat
4 tablespoons brown sugar
16 cloves
8oz (250g) shortcrust pastry
Milk for glazing
Caster sugar

Method

Peel and core the apples and stuff each with a teaspoon of mincemeat mixed with a tablespoon of sugar. Press four cloves into each apple.

Roll out the pastry and divide it into four squares, each big enough to wrap around an apple. Place an apple in the centre of each pastry square, dampen the edges with water, and fold up the corners to meet at the top, completely enclosing the apple. Place the dumplings on a greased baking tray, brush with milk and sprinkle with caster sugar. Bake in a preheated oven at 180°C (350°F) gas mark 4 for about 30 minutes. Serve with clotted cream.

APPLE IN AND OUT

Ingredients
Serves 4

8oz (225g) self-raising flour
4oz (110g) suet
6oz (175g) sugar
2 large cooking apples
A little milk

Method
Peel, core and chop the apples and mix to a fairly stiff dough with the flour, sugar, suet and milk. Place in a well-greased pudding basin, leaving plenty of room for the pudding to rise. Cover the basin with a double thickness of greaseproof paper, pleated, and steam for about 2½ hours. Turn out of the basin. Serve with clotted cream.

TO PRESERVE SWEET APPLES

Ingredients
For 4lb (1.8kg) apples

1 quart (2.3 litres) of new cider
2lb (900g) lump sugar
1 lemon
Cloves

Method
Put the cider, sugar, lemon and cloves in a large pan and bring to the boil. Peel the apples, leaving the stalks on, and simmer in the cider mixture until tender. Store in sealed jars.

EXETER PUDDING

This is just one of several recipes named after the cathedral city.

Ingredients
Serves 6-8

10oz (275g) fine white breadcrumbs
7oz (200g) suet
6oz (175g) caster sugar
7 eggs
6 ratafia biscuits
Grated rind of 1 lemon
1 tablespoon of rum
Some raisins
Jam

Methods

Beat the eggs and sugar together. Add the breadcrumbs, suet, lemon rind and rum and beat well.

Grease an ovenproof dish and line its sides with split ratafia biscuits and raisins. Spoon in layers of the egg mixture and jam. Bake in a preheated oven at 180°C (350°F) gas mark 4 for 30-40 minutes until the pudding is well-risen and firm to the touch. Serve with blackcurrant jelly melted in a little sherry.

CLOTTED CREAM

"Clowted crayme and nawe crayme put together, is eaten more for a sensuall apptyte than for any good nouryshment."

Andrew Boorde, dietician 1542.

Old spellings of the word *'clotted'* vary from clowtyd, clowted, clouted to clawted. The origins of the name are not known for sure, but a clout means a thick patch and presumably refers to the appearance of the cream as it forms.

Commercial cream production in the West Country dates back to the 13th century. Clotted cream can be sent by post to all parts of the country, indeed it was once packed in stoneware jars labelled *"To be kept dry and cool not on ice or it turns fusty."*

Method
Use a small amount of milk to begin with, increasing the amount as you become more experienced at making the cream.

Pour one pint (570ml) of creamy milk, such as Jersey, into a heavy-based saucepan. Cover and leave undisturbed in a cool place for about 12 hours in summer or 24 hours in winter.

Lift the saucepan very gently to the top of the cooker, being careful not to disturb the layer of cream which will have formed. Heat the milk on the lowest possible setting for about 45-50 minutes. On no account allow it to boil. When a solid ring of clotted cream forms around the edge of the pan, and the surface is all wrinkled, it is ready.

Remove the pan from the heat, cover again and leave in a cool place for 24 hours. Skim the cream from the pan with a slotted spoon. It is now ready to serve. The skimmed milk left in the pan can be used in baking.

DEVONSHIRE JUNKET

Devonshire junket was very popular at seaside villages, and to *"go-a-junketing"* at the weekend was a special family treat. The junket was often served with clotted cream and sprinkled with cinnamon or nutmeg. Devonshire junket is different from others as it is flavoured with brandy.

Ingredients
Serves 4-6

2 pints (1.1 litres) milk
2 tablespoons sugar
2 tablespoons brandy
2 teaspoons essence of rennet

Method
Heat the milk in a saucepan to blood heat. Stir in the sugar until dissolved. Pour the milk and sugar into the serving bowl and add the brandy. The rennet is added last of all. Cover and leave to stand at room temperature until set, about 2-3 hours, then chill in the refrigerator.

Serve spread with clotted cream, sprinkled with cinnamon or nutmeg.

WEST COUNTRY LARDER

Traditional Recipes from

CORNWALL

Compiled by Alison Ainsworth

Peninsula
Press

Published by Peninsula Press
P.O. Box 31
Newton Abbot
Devon TQ12 5XH

Editorial, Design and Production:
A&B Creative Services
Kingskerswell
Devon TQ12 5EZ
Tel: 0803 873599

Sales and Distribution:
Town & Country Books
Kingskerswell
Devon TQ12 5AZ
Tel: 0803 875875

Printed in England by Penwell Ltd, Callington, Cornwall.

The publishers would like to thank the many people of Cornwall who
have contributed to this book.

ISBN 1 872640 01 X

WEST COUNTRY LARDER
· CORNWALL ·

Contents

INTRODUCTION

Cornwall is a land of magic and superstition, where many ancient traditions persist, such as the Helston Floral or Furry Dance, performed to drive out winter's darkness and welcome in the spring. Some of these traditions are celebrated in the cookery of the county, and Helston Pudding is just one such example.

Fishing dominated the coastal towns and villages for centuries, with St Ives and Penzance being important centres for the pilchard industry. In 1871, 45,683 hogsheads of pilchards were exported, but towards the end of the century the migratory habits of the pilchard changed, and the larger shoals went elsewhere. Today, pilchards can still be caught - though in smaller numbers - in the seas around the Cornish coast, along with many other varieties of fish, providing the ingredients for dishes such as Mackerel with Soft Roe Stuffing, Marinated Pilchards and of course Starry-gazey Pie.

Life was hard for the men who worked long hours on farms, down tin mines or at sea, and it could be equally as hard for the womenfolk, looking after the home and cooking in what were often quite primitive conditions. Fuel was hard to come by, and although the local peat was cheap it was an extremely laborious task to cut and transport enough for a week's supply. In spite of this, the Cornish kitchen was - and still is - a welcoming place, with warming stews bubbling on top of the stove, and the delicate aroma of Saffron Cake or Ginger Fairings filling the air.

Fish

Scrowlers

Starry-gazey Pie

Marinated Pilchards

Potted Herrings

Cream and Anchovy Savoury

Mackerel with Soft Roe Stuffing

SCROWLERS

*"Here's a health to the Pope, may he live to repent
And add half the year to the time of his Lent
To teach all his children from Rome to the Poles
There's nothing like pilchards for saving their souls."*

Traditional

Of all the fish that provide a harvest from the seas around Cornwall, the pilchard has played the most important part in the local economy. At one time, there was such an abundance that whole villages would turn out to help land the catch. The fish were cleaned in huge brine baths, then pressed, layered in salt and packed in barrels for markets as far afield as London and Spain.

The name 'scrowler' comes from the long-handled Cornish grid iron on which the fish was cooked over an open fire.

Ingredients

*Fresh pilchards (2 or 3 per person,
depending on size and appetite!)
Salt and pepper
Cooking oil*

Method

Clean the fish and split open. Season well with salt and pepper. Heat a very little oil in a heavy based frying pan until it starts to smoke. Cook the fish quickly for a few minutes on both sides. Serve immediately with plenty of bread and butter.

STARRY-GAZEY PIE

Probably the most well-known of all Cornish fish dishes, this one is definitely not for the squeamish! Fresh sardines could be used if pilchards are not available. The fish are cooked whole, with their heads sticking up, so that there can be no doubt as to the contents of the pie!

Ingredients
Serves 6

8 pilchards or 12 good-sized sardines
8 rashers streaky bacon
1 large onion
2 heaped tablespoons chopped parsley
Salt and pepper
12oz (350g) shortcrust pastry
Milk

Method

Clean and bone the fish, or ask the fishmonger to do it for you, remembering to keep the heads on! Season the insides with salt and pepper. Peel and chop the onion, then stuff each fish with a mixture of chopped onion and parsley. Roll out the pastry and use half of it to line the base of a greased shallow pie plate or dish. Derind and chop up the bacon, then add it to the pie dish. Brush the pastry rim with milk, then lay the fish on top of the bacon, cut sides down, and with heads resting on the rim. Sprinkle over any surplus onion and parsley mixture.

Roll out the remaining pastry and use to cover the pie. Press it down firmly around the fish heads. Brush with milk and bake in a preheated oven at 200°C (400°F) gas mark 6 for 15 minutes then reduce the heat to 180°C (350°F) gas mark 4 for a further 30 minutes.

MARINATED PILCHARDS

In many fishing villages, the local baker's oven was used for cooking marinated pilchards. Each dish was covered with brown paper, on which the owner's name was written, and villagers paid a couple of pennies for the use of the oven.

Ingredients
Serves 4

8 pilchards (mackerel or herrings
could be used instead)
Salt
1 teaspoon whole black peppercorns
1 teaspoon whole cloves
1 blade mace
3 bayleaves
1/4 pint (150ml) vinegar
1/4 pint (150ml) cold tea
1 level tablespoon dark brown sugar

Method

Clean the fish, removing heads and tails. Wipe dry and salt lightly. Place in an ovenproof baking dish, packed closely together, tucking the halved bayleaves and mace in among the fish. Sprinkle with the black peppercorns and cloves. Mix together the vinegar, tea and sugar and pour over the fish.

Cover closely (but not with foil) and bake in a preheated oven at 180°C (350°F) gas mark 4, for about 50 minutes, or until the fish is tender and the bones have softened.

Marinated pilchards are excellent served cold or chilled with a little salad and some crusty bread.

POTTED HERRINGS

(Also suitable for pilchards or mackerel)

Ingredients
Serves 4

4 fresh herrings
4oz (100g) butter
1/4 pint (150ml) cider
1/2 teaspoon powdered mace
Pinch of cayenne pepper
Salt and pepper
A little melted butter

Method

Clean the fish, removing heads and tails, and place in an ovenproof dish. Add the the cider, cover, and bake in a moderate oven 180°C (350°F) gas mark 4 for about 30 minutes. Let it cool slightly, then lift the fish out of the cooking liquid and remove bones and skin. Liquidise the flesh or mash well with a fork, then place in a saucepan with the butter, mace and cayenne pepper. Heat slowly, stirring so that everything is well mixed together. Season with salt and pepper. When the mixture comes to the boil, remove from the heat and pour into a jar (or jars). Seal the top with melted butter. Store in a fridge, and eat straight away, once the butter seal has been broken. Delicious spread on toast.

CREAM AND ANCHOVY SAVOURY

A highly unusual - and deliciously different - way to start a special dinner party.

Ingredients
Serves 6

6 slices of white bread, about 1/2" (1.5cm) thick
A 1 ½oz (45g) tin of anchovy fillets
2oz (50g) butter
6 tablespoons Cornish clotted cream, chilled

Method

Cut the bread into squares about 2½" (6.5cm) across, or use a large biscuit cutter to make six rounds. Melt the butter in a frying pan and fry the bread until it is golden. Place the fried bread on a serving plate, lay three anchovy fillets, well-drained, on each portion, and top with a tablespoon of clotted cream.

MACKEREL WITH SOFT ROE STUFFING

Only the soft roes of the fish should be used in this recipe.

Ingredients
Serves 4

4 medium mackerel with soft roes
2 anchovy fillets or 1 teaspoon anchovy essence
2oz (50g) soft white breadcrumbs

2oz (50g) butter
1 medium onion
1 heaped tablespoon chopped parsley and chives
Grated rind of half a lemon
1 tablespoon lemon juice
A little milk
Salt and freshly ground black pepper
1oz (25g) butter for greasing the dish

Method

Ask your fishmonger to clean the fish and remove the backbones. Melt the butter and cook the roes for barely two minutes, then lift them out and add the chopped onion. Cover the pan and let the onion soften over a gentle heat. While the onion is cooking, mix the breadcrumbs with the milk, then chop the roes roughly and add them to the softened onion, together with the bread mixture, grated lemon rind, chopped anchovies (or anchovy essence) and herbs. Fill the fish with this mixture, and pack them into a greased ovenproof dish or shallow casserole. Bake in a preheated oven at 220°C (425°F) gas mark 7 according to the size of the fish, allowing about 10 minutes for each inch of thickness.

" ...We had for dinner some boiled tench eels fryed etc all which Mrs Custance sent us last night after their return home which was very, very kind indeed of them ..."

From The Diary of a Country Parson, by the Rev. James Woodforde

Meat & Vegetables

Kiddly Broth

Likky Pie

Cornish Pasties

Likky Pasties

Stewed Beef with Vegetables

Potato Cake

KIDDLY BROTH

Also known as Kettle Broth because of the pot in which it was cooked, this humble soup was made from whatever ingredients were to hand. For the poorest farm worker and his family, this often meant no more than a handful of herbs and some seasoning, boiled together in water, then poured over chunks of stale bread in individual bowls. Marigold petals were often sprinkled on top for their medicinal value, and the bright orange and yellow flowers would have brightened up an otherwise dreary meal.

Ingredients
Serves 6

8oz (225g) leeks
1 large onion
2 pints (1.1 litres) stock
1/2 pint (275ml) milk
1 ½oz (40g) butter or margarine
6 slices cut from a French stick
1 freshly picked marigold head
Salt and pepper

Method
Melt the butter or margarine in a large saucepan then soften the peeled and chopped onion and leeks in it over a very gentle heat, for about 15 minutes. Add the stock, salt and pepper, and simmer, covered, for about 25 minutes. Liquidise in a food processor or pass through a sieve, then return the mixture to the saucepan, add the milk and heat through gently.

Put the slices of bread into individual warmed bowls, pour the soup over and decorate with marigold petals.

LIKKY PIE

'Likky' is the traditional term for leeks in Cornwall.

Ingredients
Serves 4-6

10 leeks, cleaned and sliced
6oz (175g) unsmoked bacon rashers
1/4 pint (150ml) cream
1/4 pint (150ml) milk
8oz (225g) shortcrust pastry
2 eggs, separated
Salt and pepper

Method
Simmer the leeks in the milk, seasoned, for 5 minutes, then lift out with a serrated spoon and layer with the rashers of bacon in a greased pie dish. Pour over the milk, then roll out the pastry and cover the pie dish with it. Use any leftover pastry to decorate the top with leaves, etc. Bake in a preheated oven at 190°C (375°F) gas mark 5 for 30 minutes. Remove from the oven and carefully lift off the pastry lid. Take out some of the liquid. Beat together the egg yolks and cream, then fold in the stiffly beaten egg whites. Spread this mixture on top of the pie, replace the pastry lid and return to the oven for a further 10 minutes.

CORNISH PASTIES

"Pastry rolled out like a plate,
Piled with turmut, tates and mate,
Doubled up and baked like fate,
That's a Cornish Pasty!"

Traditional

Long famed as the staple dish of the region, the pasty evolved from the agricultural poverty of Cornwall, at about the end of the eighteenth century. It was a good way to stretch a small amount of meat to feed a large family. The first pasties often consisted of vegetables in a dark barley corn crust, and instead of being baked they were sometimes wrapped in a cabbage leaf and steamed over broth or anything else that happened to be boiling in a pot over the fire. Traditionally pasties were eaten in the hand and never cut with a knife and fork.

Men working in the fields, fishermen on boats, workers in tin mines, all lived on pasties, and because the pasties were much larger than those made nowadays, they lasted all day and would be marked with the owner's initials at one corner, so that if left down they could be retrieved without any doubt as to their rightful owner.

Ingredients
Makes 4 pasties

1lb (450g) shortcrust pastry
12oz (350g) chuck steak, cut into small cubes
3 medium potatoes, peeled and chopped
1 medium onion, peeled and diced
4oz (110g) swede, peeled and diced
Salt and pepper
Egg or milk for glazing

Method

Roll out the pastry and cut into 8" (20cm) rounds, using a plate as a guide. Mix all of the ingredients (apart from the egg or milk) together and divide equally among the pastry rounds, putting the mixture on one half only. Moisten the edges of the pastry with water and fold the uncovered halves of the pastry over to make a half moon shape. Pinch and crimp the edges to gave a rope effect. Make a few slits for the steam to escape, then place the pasties on a greased baking sheet and brush with milk or beaten egg.

Bake in a preheated oven at 200°C (400°F) gas mark 6 for 15 minutes. Then turn the heat down to 180°C (350°F) gas mark 4 for a further 40 minutes. Equally delicious served hot or cold.

LIKKY PASTIES

Ingredients
Makes 4 pasties

1lb (450g) shortcrust pastry
2 large leeks
4 rashers bacon
1 egg
Milk
Salt and pepper

Method

Wash the leeks and chop finely. Derind the bacon and chop into small pieces, then mix with the leeks and the egg, beaten, saving some of the egg for brushing the pastry. Proceed as in the previous pasty recipe, placing equal quantities of the leek and bacon mixture on the four rounds of pastry.

STEWED BEEF WITH VEGETABLES

Before the introduction of gas and electric cookers, most Cornish meals were cooked on top of the fire or stove, as it was hard to find sufficient fuel to make a hot oven.

"I was surprised to find my supper boyling on a fire allwayes supply'd with a bush of furze and that to be the only fewell to dress a joynt of meat and broth, and told them they could not roast me anything, but they have a little wood for such occasions but its scarce and dear - which is a strange thing that the shipps could not supply them, they told me it must all be brought round the Land End, and since the warre they could not have it . . ."

Celia Fiennes, 1698

Ingredients
Serves 4

1lb (450g) chuck or shin steak, cubed
1 large onion, sliced
2 large carrots, peeled and sliced
1 small swede, peeled and chopped
2 parsnips, peeled and chopped
2 large potatoes, peeled and sliced
Salt and pepper

Method
Put the beef in a large saucepan and cover with the sliced onion. Pour over enough cold water to cover, season with salt and pepper and bring to simmering point. Now add the carrots, swede and parsnips, finishing with a layer of potatoes.

Cover and cook over a gentle heat until the meat is tender (about 2 -3 hours), adding more water as required. Take care not to stir the stew or the vegetables will become mushy.

POTATO CAKE

It was the custom to cook more potatoes than were needed so that there were always plenty left over to be fried in dripping, or made into these delicious cakes, usually known as 'tatie cakes'.

Ingredients
Serves 4

8oz (225g) cold, mashed potatoes
4oz (110g) butter or dripping
4oz (110g) lightly cooked, chopped bacon
1 teaspoon baking powder
Flour
Salt

Method

Rub the butter or dripping into the potatoes and add sufficient flour to make a firm paste. Mix in the other ingredients and shape into a round cake about 1" (2.5 cm) thick. Place on a greased baking sheet and bake at 200°C (400°F) gas mark 6 for 30 minutes. Serve hot.

Cakes &
Puddings

Heavy Cake
Saffron Cake
Cornish Splits
Ginger Fairings
Cornish Clotted Cream
West Country Tarts
Helston Pudding
Baked Figgy Pudding

HEAVY CAKE

This cake was first made in Cornish fishing ports, where 'hevva' was the name given to the hauling in of the fish. The top of the cake was always decorated with a criss-cross pattern, to represent a fishing net. To make an even richer cake, replace the butter with 1 pint (570ml) clotted cream and a well-beaten egg.

Ingredients

1lb (450g) plain flour
12oz (350g) butter
6oz (175g) currants
2oz (50g) sugar
Pinch of salt
Cold water to mix
Milk for glazing

Method

Mix the flour and salt together in a large bowl. Cut the butter into three equal portions and rub one of the portions into the flour. Mix to a stiff dough with a little water. Knead in the currants and sugar, then roll out the dough on a floured board. Cut the second portion of butter into small pieces and strew them over the dough. Sprinkle with flour and fold the dough in half. Turn the dough and roll it out again. Do the same thing with the third portion of butter, finally rolling out the dough until it is about 1" (2.5cm) thick. Form the dough into an oval shape, then make a criss-cross pattern on top using the blade of a knife. Place on a greased baking sheet, brush with milk and bake in a preheated oven at 220°C (425°F) gas mark 7 for about 30 minutes.

SAFFRON CAKE

The strong yellow spice, Saffron, was probably first introduced to Cornwall by the Phoenicians, who traded it (and other spices) for Cornish tin.

Ingredients

1lb (450g) plain flour
4oz (110g) butter or margarine
4oz (110g) lard
2oz (50g) sugar
6oz (175g) currants
2oz (50g) sultanas
1oz (25g) mixed chopped peel
1/2oz (10g) dried yeast mixed
with 1/2 level tablespoon sugar
1/4 pint (150ml) warm milk
1/4 - 1/2 teaspoon powdered saffron

Method

Infuse the saffron in a bowl with about 1/4 pint (150ml) boiling water and leave overnight. Mix the yeast and sugar with half of the warm milk, then put aside until frothy (about 15 minutes). Sieve the flour and salt into a mixing bowl and rub in the butter or margarine finely. Stir in the sugar, currants, sultanas and peel. Make a well in the centre and pour in the yeast mixture, the saffron water and sufficient milk to mix to a soft dough. Cover with clingfilm and leave in a warm place until double in size. Grease a 2lb (900g) loaf tin and line with greaseproof paper. Knead the risen dough on a floured board, making sure there are no air bubbles trapped in the mixture. Place the dough in the tin and leave for 30 minutes or so, then bake in a preheated oven at 180°C (350°F) gas mark 4 for 1½ hours. The cake is ready when a skewer inserted in the middle comes out clean.

CORNISH SPLITS

The Cornish have always made good use of their clotted cream, particularly at tea time, when it is spread liberally on bread, scones and Cornish Splits. 'Thunder and Lightning' is the name given to Splits spread first with cream and then with golden syrup - a firm favourite, particularly with children.

Ingredients
Makes 18 Splits

For the yeast mixture:

4oz (110g) strong white flour
About 1/3 pint (175ml) warm water
1oz (25g) fresh yeast
1/2oz (10g) sugar
1 large egg

For the dough:

14oz (400g) strong white flour
3oz (75g) sugar
2oz (50g) butter, left at room temperature
1/4 teaspoon salt

Method for the yeast mixture:

Beat the egg, then mix it with enough warm water to make 1/2 pint (275ml) of liquid. Mix the yeast to a smooth paste with a little of this liquid (about 3 tablespoons), then add the rest of the liquid, and whisk in the flour and sugar to make a smooth batter. Cover and leave in a warm place to rise for about 30 minutes.

Method for the dough:

Sieve the flour and salt into a large mixing bowl and make a well in the middle. Put the sugar in the well and pour in the yeast mixture. Stir until the sugar is dissolved, then gradually mix in the flour to make a soft and sticky dough. Knead the butter into the dough until it is smooth. Shape into a ball, put in a warmed, greased bowl, covered with cling film, and leave to rise in a warm place for about 45 minutes.

Turn out the dough, and divide it into 18 pieces. Form the pieces into balls and leave to rest for five minutes. Now roll out the balls to make 3" (7.5cm) rounds. Fold the rounds in half and place them on a warmed and greased baking sheet, leaving plenty of space around each one. Cover with greased polythene and leave in a warm place to rise for a further 40 minutes. Remove the polythene and bake in a preheated oven at 230°C (450°F) gas mark 8 for 10 minutes.

When the splits have cooled, break them open, fill with jam and cream, and dust with icing sugar.

GINGER FAIRINGS

Fairs attracted vast crowds of people, whether to buy or sell, have fun on the rides and amusements, meet up with old friends or indeed take on a labourer or house maid. Launceston was the site for a 'maid hiring fair' which took place every year, just after Christmas; a Gooseberry Fair was held annually in Helston, and there was a Strawberry Fair at Penzance. Among the wide array of home made sweets and cakes on sale would be these delicious crisp biscuits.

Ingredients
Makes about 18

8oz (225g) plain flour
4oz (110g) butter or margarine
4oz (110g) caster sugar
4 tablespoons golden syrup
3 level teaspoons ground ginger
2 level teaspoons baking powder
2 level teaspoons bicarbonate of soda
2 level teaspoons ground mixed spice
1 level teaspoon ground cinnamon
1/2 teaspoon salt

Method
Sieve together all of the dry ingredients except for the sugar, then rub in the butter or margarine until the mixture resembles fine breadcrumbs. Stir in the sugar. Heat the syrup gently and add it to the mixture, stirring thoroughly. The mixture should be fairly stiff.

Roll the mixture into small balls the size of walnuts. (You may find this easier to do if you flour your hands first.) Place the balls on a greased baking tray, leaving plenty of room for the Fairings to spread out. Bake near the top of a preheated oven at 200°C (400°F) gas mark 6 for no more than 10-12 minutes. Halfway through the baking time, or as soon as the Fairings start to brown, move the tray to the bottom of the oven. Remove from the oven and leave to cool for a few minutes before transferring to a wire tray with a spatula. Leave until completely cold. Store in an airtight tin.

CORNISH CLOTTED CREAM

Commercial cream production in the West Country dates back to the 13th century. The cream used to be packed into stoneware jars on the side of which was the inscription *"To be kept dry and cool, not on ice or it turns fusty."* Cornish clotted cream is usually thicker and more yellow in colour than its Devonian counterpart.

"This cream is so much esteemed that it is sent to the London markets in small square tins and jars, and is exceedingly delicate eaten with fresh fruit."

Mrs Beeton

WEST COUNTRY TARTS

"... thence I went over the heath and commons by the tinn mines, to St. Austins [St. Austell] *which is a little market town ... here was a pretty good dineing-room and chamber within it, and very neate country women; my Landlady brought me one of the West Country tarts, this was the first I met with, though I had asked for them in many places in Sommerset and Devonshire, its an apple pye with a custard all on the top, its the most acceptable entertainment that could be made me; they scald their creame and milk in most parts of those countrys and so its a sort of clouted cream as we call it, with a little sugar, and soe put on the top of the apple pye; I was much pleased with my supper ... "*

Celia Fiennes 1698

HELSTON PUDDING

The town of Helston is famous for the Helston Floral or Furry Dance which is thought to be one of the oldest spring festival dances in the country. Each year on May 8th, dancers process through the streets of the town, dancing into shops and private homes, through the front door and out at the back. This was thought to bring the shopkeeper and householders good luck, by letting in the sun and driving out the winter darkness.

Ingredients
Serves 6

2oz (50g) flour
2oz (50g) suet
2oz (50g) sugar
2oz (50g) ground rice
2oz (50g) breadcrumbs
2oz (50g) raisins
2oz (50g) currants
1/2 teacup milk
1/2 teaspoon bicarbonate of soda
1/2 teaspoon mixed spice
A little chopped mixed peel
Pinch of salt

Method
Dissolve the bicarbonate of soda in the milk. Mix all of the dry ingredients together, then stir in the milk. Transfer to a well-buttered pudding basin and cover with a double thickness of greaseproof paper, pleated to allow for expansion, and secured with string.

Steam in a large saucepan for two hours, topping up with boiling water if necessary. Serve hot with Cornish clotted cream or custard.

BAKED FIGGY PUDDING

Contrary to its name, there are no figs in this dish - 'figgy' being the old Cornish word for 'raisin'. This substantial pudding was often served at 'gulldize', the name given to the hot midday meal provided by the farmer's wife for threshing crews during harvest.

Ingredients
Serves 4-6

12oz (350g) mixed dried fruit and peel
8oz (225g) self raising flour
4oz (110g) suet
4oz (110g) breadcrumbs
2 large eggs
2 level tablespoons brown sugar
1 teaspoon mixed spice
Milk
Pinch of salt

Method
Mix all the ingredients together, adding a little milk if the mixture seems too stiff. Transfer to a greased ovenproof dish and bake in a preheated oven at 150°C (300°F) gas mark 2 for 2 hours. Serve hot.

Drinks

Cornish Mead
Spruce
Mahogany
Egg'yot
Sampson

CORNISH MEAD

Legend has it that King Arthur and his Knights of the Round Table drank mead when they met at Tintagel in North Cornwall. There are several different recipes for Cornish mead, which at one time was brewed in many villages throughout the county.

Ingredients
Makes 8 pints (4.5 litres)

8 pints (4.5 litres) water
3lb (1.35kg) clear honey
Juice and thinly peeled rind of 2 lemons
2oz (50g) fresh root ginger
1oz (25g) fresh yeast

Method

Put the honey in a warm place until its temperature reaches 50°C (122°F). Bruise the ginger by wrapping it in a clean cloth and hitting it with a meat tenderiser or hammer. This helps to release the flavour. Now tie the ginger and the lemon peel in a square of muslin and place in a large saucepan, or preserving pan. Add the water and lemon juice and bring to the boil, then turn off the heat and allow to cool to 50°C (122°F), the same temperature as the honey.

Stir the honey into the water mixture and allow it to cool to 21°C (70 °F). Remove the ginger and lemon peel. Crumble the yeast and add to the mixture. Pour the liquid into an 8 pint (4.5 litre) fermentation jar, until the jar is three-quarters full, and fit an airlock. This keeps out air but allows fermentation gases to escape. The yeast will slowly sink to the bottom of the jar. It will be necessary to 'rack' the mead, i.e. siphon the clear liquid into a clean fermentation jar, discarding the yeast sediment. This may need to be done more than once, so that the mead is clear, and to ensure that the fermentation process has finished.

Leave the mead for about 2 weeks before transferring to bottles with secure plastic or cork stoppers. The mead should be stored in a cool, dark place and may be drunk after 5 months but is even better if kept for several years.

SPRUCE

This drink no longer includes the sap of the spruce tree, as it did in the 17th century , when spruce beer was drunk to purify the blood. In later years, the main ingredients were lemon and sugar and it was particularly popular with farm workers especially at harvest time.

Ingredients
Makes 7 pints (4 litres)

12oz (350g) sugar
1 lemon
6 pints (4 litres) cold water
1 pint (570ml) boiling water
2 teaspoons tartaric acid
2 teaspoons ground ginger

Method
Peel the lemon thinly and squeeze out the juice. Put the sugar in a bowl together with the lemon rind, lemon juice, tartaric acid and ginger. Pour over the boiling water and stir until the sugar has dissolved. Leave until cool, then add the cold water. Chill, and remove the lemon rind. Serve with ice and lemon slices.

MAHOGANY

This was a favourite drink with Cornish fishermen, who thought it the ideal drink to accompany pilchards. In 1781 Dr Johnson and Boswell were served Mahogany at a dinner party given by Sir Joshua Reynolds. Boswell wrote:

> "I thought it very good liquor: a counterpart of what is
> called Atholl Porridge in the Highlands of Scotland,
> which is a mixture of whisky and honey!"

Ingredients and method

Simply combine one cup of treacle with two cups of gin, and beat well together. Quantities can be varied according to the amount required.

EGG'YOT

> "A Happy New Year, and a young woman,
> And plenty of money with your wife!"
>
> Old Cornish toast.

Ingredients

Makes about 2 pints (1.1 litres)

2 pints (1.1 litres) beer
2 eggs
2 tablespoons sugar

Method

Simply beat the eggs and sugar together, then heat the beer in a saucepan and stir the egg and sugar mixture into it. Serve hot.

SAMPSON

A variation on the previous recipe, cider is the main ingredient here. Sampson is said to be very good for curing a cold!

Ingredients
Makes about 2 pints (1.1 litres)

2 pints (1.1 litres) cider
2 eggs
2 tablespoons sugar

Method

Beat the eggs and sugar together, then heat the cider in a saucepan and stir the egg and sugar mixture into it. Serve hot.

WEST COUNTRY LARDER

Traditional Recipes from

SOMERSET

Compiled by Alison Ainsworth and Linda Clements

Peninsula
Press

Published by Peninsula Press
P.O. Box 31
Newton Abbot
Devon TQ12 5XH

Editorial, Design and Production:
A&B Creative Services
Kingskerswell
Devon TQ12 5EZ
Tel: 0803 873599

Sales and Distribution:
Town & Country Books
Kingskerswell
Devon TQ12 5AZ
Tel: 0803 875875

Printed in England by Penwell Ltd, Callington, Cornwall.

The publishers would like to thank the many people of Somerset who
have contributed to this book.

ISBN 1 872640 02 8

WEST COUNTRY LARDER
· SOMERSET ·

Contents

INTRODUCTION

The landscape of Somerset ranges from gently rolling hills and valleys to wild and vivid heathlands. The peaty soil of the levels, which have been reclaimed from the sea, provide excellent grazing for sheep. Cows feeding on lush pasture land have produced the rich milk, cream, butter and cheese at the centre of Somerset cookery.

Somerset is a land of legend and tradition, famous in particular for its Cheddar cheese, the name taken from a town south of the Mendip Hills. This much imitated cheese has been made the same way for hundreds of years.

Somerset has about forty miles of coastline and in the past has enjoyed a rich harvest from the sea, with tenacious fishermen bringing home varied catches including herring, mackerel, turbot and mullet.

The fertile valleys of southern Somerset provide a varied fare - onions, watercress, celery, carrots, leeks, walnuts, strawberries, gooseberries and the most important crop of all, apples - dessert, cooker and cider. To many folk Somerset *is* cider.

Starters

Watercress Soup

Somerset Rarebit

Mussels with Saffron

Oxtail Soup

West Country Pâté

Cheese Straws

WATERCRESS SOUP

This delicious soup may be served hot or chilled in summer and garnished with sprigs of watercress.

Ingredients
Serves 4

8oz (225g) chopped watercress
8oz (225g) potatoes
2 small onions
1oz (25g) butter
1 pint (570ml) water
1 ‡ pints (850ml) milk
1oz (25g) finely grated Cheddar cheese
1/4 pint (150ml) double cream
1/2 teaspoon nutmeg
Salt and pepper

Method

Remove thick stalks and discoloured leaves from watercress, wash well and drain. Peel and slice potatoes and onions, place in the water, bring to the boil and simmer for 15 minutes or until soft. Rub potatoes and onions through a sieve, saving the cooking liquid. Melt the butter in a saucepan, add watercress and cook gently for about 3 minutes, without browning. Stir in potato and onion mixture, add the milk and the water in which the vegetables were boiled. Simmer for 15 minutes. Rub through a sieve or liquidise in a blender. Reheat the soup, stir in the nutmeg and seasoning. Blend in the cream and sprinkle the cheese on top before serving .

SOMERSET RAREBIT

The origins of this dish date back to eighteenth century Wales. Other regions have their own version, incoporating local cheeses, and of course Somerset rarebit is made with tasty Cheddar cheese.

Ingredients
Serves 8 as a savoury start to a meal
or 4 as a light snack.

8oz (225g) Cheddar cheese
1oz (25g) plain flour
1oz (25g) butter
1 teaspoon dry mustard
2 tablespoons dry cider or beer
2 tomatoes
4 rounds of buttered toast
Salt and pepper

Method

Melt the butter in saucepan, stir in the flour and mustard, then add the cider, stirring continuously. Grate the Cheddar and mix in, cooking gently until the cheese melts. Season to taste. Spread the cheese mixture onto the freshly made buttered toast. Slice the tomatoes and lay slices on top of the cheese. Brown under a hot grill until the cheese is bubbling. Cut into 8 pieces if required as a starter and serve hot.

MUSSELS WITH SAFFRON

Porlock Weir, which means 'enclosed harbour', was a herring port until the eighteenth century and until 1910 had an oyster fishery. Small mussels are still found on Porlock Weir beach.

Ingredients
Serves 4 as a starter.

About 24 mussels
2 onions
2 leeks
7oz (200g) tin tomatoes
1 glass white wine
Juice of half a lemon
1 clove of garlic
Sprig of thyme
1 bay leaf
Pinch of saffron
A little chopped parsley
Olive oil
Salt and pepper

Method

Heat olive oil in a shallow pan, add chopped onions, the finely sliced white part of the leeks, chopped garlic, bay leaf, thyme, parsley and saffron. Cook gently until softened, then add tomatoes, white wine, lemon juice and seasoning. Continue cooking until the sauce is thick and sticky. Place the cleaned mussels in a flat pan, pour the sauce over, then cover and cook over a brisk heat for about 5 minutes. Serve with chunks of fresh crusty bread.

OXTAIL SOUP

Simple but nourishing, a good broth played an important part in the diet of country folk, and indeed was often the main meal of the day in poorer households. This recipe follows the true West Country tradition of using every part of the cow except for its moo!

Ingredients
Serves 4-6

1 meaty oxtail, divided into joints
2oz (50g) dripping or oil
2 onions, peeled and chopped
2 carrots, peeled and chopped
3 sticks celery, trimmed and chopped
3 pints (1.7litres) beef stock
4 tablespoons sherry
3 bay leaves and a bouquet garni
2 tablespoons plain flour
1/4 teaspoon grated nutmeg
Salt and pepper

Method
Soak oxtail in water for 4 hours, then drain. Heat dripping or oil in a large saucepan, add oxtail pieces, browning all over. Remove oxtail and cook onions, carrots and celery in the pan over a medium heat, until onions are golden brown. Return oxtail to the pan, add the stock, bay leaves, bouquet garni and seasoning. Simmer for 3 hours, then remove bay leaves, bouquet garni and oxtail. Remove meat from the bones and put back into soup. Mix flour with a little water and use to thicken the soup. Lastly, add nutmeg and sherry and season to taste. Allow to cool to remove excess fat, then reheat to serve.

WEST COUNTRY PÂTÉ

The Old English term for the French word pâté is 'potted' meaning a smooth or coarse rich paste. Meat has been potted, primarily to preserve it, since the middle ages.

Ingredients
Serves 12

1lb (450g) pork or pork sausagemeat
1lb (450g) chicken livers
8oz (225g) streaky bacon
1 onion
1-2 cloves garlic, crushed
2 tablespoons double cream
2 tablespoons brandy
1/2 teaspoon dried thyme
1/2 teaspoon freshly ground black pepper
1/2 teaspoon salt

Method
Remove the rind from the bacon and use it to line the bottom of a 2lb (900g) loaf tin or a 2 pint (1.1litre) ovenproof dish. Chop up the pork, onion and chicken liver, mix and put through a mincer. Stir in salt, pepper, thyme, garlic, brandy and cream. Pack mixture into tin, cover with a foil lid and cook at 170°C (325°F) gas mark 3 for 2 hours. Remove from oven, leave in tin, with weight on top of pâté for 8 hours or overnight in the fridge. Before serving, remove weight and turn out onto a plate, or serve from dish.

CHEESE STRAWS

Cheddar is famous not only for its spectacular caves of stalagmites and stalactites at Cheddar Gorge, but also for its much imitated cheese, and some of the best Cheddar cheese is made in nearby Castle Cary.

These cheese straws are tasty little sticks, simple to make, and can be served as a cocktail snack or in napkin rings to accompany clear soup.

Ingredients
Makes about 48

4oz (110g) finely grated Cheddar cheese
3oz (75g) butter or margarine
3oz (75g) plain flour
1 egg, separated
1/2 teaspoon mustard powder
Pinch of salt
Pinch of cayenne powder

Method
Cream the cheese and butter together, stir in the sifted flour, mustard powder, salt and cayenne. Then add the beaten egg yolk and mix into a stiff dough. On a lightly floured surface roll the dough to 1/4" (5mm) thick, then cut into strips about 4" (10cm) long, 1/4" (5mm) wide. Place on a greased baking tray, brush with beaten egg white and bake in a preheated oven at 200°C (400°F) gas mark 6, for about 10 minutes.

Main Courses

Fisherman's Pie

Stuffed Herrings

West Buckland Trout

Jugged Hare

Somerset Braised Lamb

Pig's Head Brawn

Somerset Pork with Cider Cream Sauce

Braised Beef and Prunes Stuffed with Walnuts

Samphire Hash

To Make a Herbe Pudding

FISHERMAN'S PIE

This dish makes use of two local ingredients - fresh haddock and dry cider.

Ingredients
Serves 4-6

1lb (450g) haddock fillet, lightly poached
14oz (400g) frozen puff pastry
4oz (110g) cooked peas
3 hard boiled eggs
1/2 pint (275ml) dry cider
1/4 pint (150ml) milk
1 ½oz (40g) butter
1 ½oz (40g) plain flour
Salt and pepper

Method

Thaw pastry and roll out to a rectangle about 11"x 8" (28cm x 20cm). Mark out another rectangle about 1" (25mm) from the edge to form a 'lid'. Do not cut right through. Brush with egg or milk and bake in a preheated oven 220°C (425°F) gas mark 7 for 20-25 minutes. Remove the 'lid'. Melt the butter in a pan and add the flour, cooking for a minute. Remove from the heat and gradually stir in the dry cider and milk. Return to the heat, stirring continuously, bring to the boil and cook for a minute. Flake the haddock, chop the eggs and add to the sauce with the peas and seasoning. Pour mixture into pastry case, put 'lid' on top and if necessary reheat in the oven for about 15 minutes at 190°C (375°F) gas mark 5.

STUFFED HERRINGS

Traditionally known as the 'poor man's fish', herrings are extremely nutritious. In the days when herring shoals were plentiful, the fish were sold from large earthenware pans and housewives took them home in their own dishes.

Ingredients
Serves 4

4 herrings
1 small onion
4oz (110g) cottage or cream cheese
2oz (50g) double cream
1/2 pint (275ml) cider
Cucumber slices
Salt and pepper

Method

Clean the herrings and cut off tails, fins and heads, then split the fish down the back. Remove the soft roes and mash them. Peel and chop the onion finely. Whip the cream until thick. Mix the cream, onion, roes and seasoning. Insert this stuffing into the split backs of the fish and place them in a frying pan. Pour the cider over the fish, bring to the boil and poach slowly until cooked, turning fish carefully once. Remove the fish and keep warm on a serving dish. Meanwhile allow the cider liquid to cool, then beat in the cheese to form a sauce. Pour over the fish and garnish with thin cucumber slices.

WEST BUCKLAND TROUT

West Buckland is a pretty village near Wellington in Somerset, and like many places in the West Country where the water is pure, fresh-water trout are a popular delicacy. Izaak Walton, writing of the trout's fondness for the mayfly, said *"These make the trout bold and lusty, and he is usually fatter and better meat at the end of May, than at any time of the year."*

Ingredients
Serves 4

4 small trout
1 ½lb (700g) mushrooms
6oz (175g) butter
4 slices of bread
1 teaspoon dried tarragon
Parsley
Slices of lemon
Flour
Salt and pepper

Method

Gut the trout and remove the tails and heads. Mash the tarragon with 2oz (50g) butter, season, and place inside the fish. Coat the fish in seasoned flour and wrap in greaseproof paper. Place under a hot grill and cook until the paper chars. Meanwhile, chop the mushrooms finely and fry gently in 2oz (50g) butter. Season. Then fry the slices of bread in the remaining butter until golden brown. Unwrap the trout and arrange it on the bread with the mushrooms. Pour the pan juices over the fish and serve, garnished with parsley and lemon slices.

JUGGED HARE

In the land of Lorna Doone and wild Exmoor, Jugged Hare was traditional fare for Boxing Day dinner.

Ingredients
Serves 4

1 medium sized hare cut into joints
6 rashers bacon
2 medium onions
3 carrots
2 sticks celery
1 wineglass red wine or port
3 tablespoons redcurrant jelly
4 tablespoons of oil
1 teaspoon each of parsley, thyme and marjoram
2 bayleaves
2 heaped tablespoons of flour

The marinade:
1 onion, sliced
1 glass red wine or cider
1 glass of wine/cider vinegar
2 tablespoons olive oil
6 juniper berries, crushed
2 bayleaves
Sprig of rosemary
Salt and pepper

Method
Combine the marinade ingredients, cover the hare joints and leave to marinade for 4 hours or overnight. Remove from the marinade, dry

slightly and brown in a pan with the oil. Chop the vegetables and put them in an ovenproof dish. Add the hare joints, cover with the bacon and scatter the herbs and flour over the top. Season, and add the marinade, topping up with water if necessary. Cover and cook in a preheated oven at 150°C (300°F) gas mark 2 for about 2½ hours. Stir in the wine and redcurrant jelly, and cook, uncovered, for a further 30 minutes.

SOMERSET BRAISED LAMB

Jacob's sheep are a black and white sheep traditionally associated with the town of Yeovil. There is a thriving sheepskin industry and the meat from the young lambs lends itself well to many delicious recipes.

Ingredients
Serves about 8

4lb (1.8kg) leg or best end neck of lamb
3 carrots
3 turnips
2 leeks
1 large onion
1/2 pint (250ml) cider
1 tablespoon currants
1 tablespoon sultanas or seedless raisins
1 tablespoon oil
3 bayleaves
3 cloves
6 black peppercorns, pinch of salt

Method

In a large saucepan put the lamb, bayleaves, cloves, peppercorns and enough water to half cover the joint, cover and simmer for 30 minutes. Meanwhile, heat the oil in an ovenproof dish and sauté the chopped vegetables until they are soft, but not browned. Place the lamb on top with 1/2 pint of the cooking liquid, strained and the cider. Add the fruit, cloves and salt, then cover and bake in a moderate oven at 180°C (350°F) gas mark 4 for 2½ hours. To serve, place the joint in a dish and arrange the vegetables around it.

PIG'S HEAD BRAWN

"Take one pig's head, wash and clean thoroughly and put in a basin with plenty of water and two handfuls of salt and a piece of saltpetre. Leave it all night, then rinse well put it in a boiling pot and cover it with cold water. Boil for two hours or until the meat leaves the bone easily, then cut it up in small pieces, also the ears and tongue (after skinning the tongue). Return the bones to the boiling liquid, together with some carrots, an onion, twelve allspice berries, a bunch of herbs, some turnips, shallots, five peppercorns and five cloves. Boil for about one hour until greatly reduced. Strain the liquor into another pot. Put in the pieces of meat, season as required and bring to the boil. Rinse a mould with cold water, and pour in the meat and liquor. Leave in a cold place to set."

Traditional recipe from Frome.

SOMERSET PORK WITH CIDER CREAM SAUCE

Somerset farmer's wives have used cider in cooking for generations, and it combines particularly well with pork. Cider can usually be substituted for wine in most recipes.

Ingredients
Serves 4

1-1 ½lb (700g) pork fillet or 8 thin pork steaks
2oz (50g) butter
1 large onion, chopped
6oz (175g) mushrooms, sliced
1/2 pint (250ml) dry cider
4 tablespoons double cream
2 level tablespoons flour
Salt and pepper

Method

Cut pork fillet into 8 pieces and beat each piece between greaseproof paper with a meat hammer or rolling pin until about 1/4" (5mm) thick. Coat the pieces with flour and fry slowly in the butter for about 3 minutes on each side. Drain and keep warm. Add onions and mushrooms to pan and cook gently until tender. Stir in remaining flour and cook for a minute. Remove from heat and gradually stir in the cider. Return to the heat and, stirring all the time, cook for a minute. Add the pork pieces and seasoning, finally stirring in the cream. Heat but do not boil. Serve garnished with fresh parsley.

BRAISED BEEF AND PRUNES STUFFED WITH WALNUTS

The Vale of Pewsey in Somerset is known for its walnut trees which provide an unusual ingredient for this recipe. This is also good with pork chops or rabbit.

Ingredients
Serves 4-6

3lb (1.3kg) lean stewing beef, cubed
1 large onion, sliced
10 prunes, soaked overnight
10 walnut halves
1/2 pint (250ml) dark beer or stout
4 cloves
1 garlic clove, chopped
1 heaped tablespoon flour
Salt and pepper

Method

Heat the oil and lightly brown the meat. Add the onion and cook until soft. Shake the flour over the beef and onion and mix well, then add the cloves, garlic, seasoning and beer. Allow the mixture to boil and if the sauce is too thick add water or stock. Transfer to an ovenproof casserole, cover and braise in a preheated oven at 150°C (300°F) gas mark 2 for about 2 hours. Stone the prunes and stuff with the walnut halves, then add to the casserole. Continue cooking for a further 30 minutes, uncovered.

SAMPHIRE HASH

This sauce was poured over tough beef to make it more tender. The blue-green samphire and scarlet barberries made a stunning garnish.

"Take some samphire, a handful of pickled cucumbers and some capers, and chop altogether with vinegar and strong broth. Add a lemon cut into pieces, nutmeg and pepper. Let it boyle then thicken with butter and yolk of an egg and a little sugar. Pour over the meat and decorate with samphire and barberries."

From a 17th century recipe.

TO MAKE A HERBE PUDDING

"Take new milke as it comes from ye cow and a topenny manchet [loaf of bread] and soak together all night then scueese out ye milke and take egg whites and beat together then put them to ye bread with a deale of origanum and two or three tops of sweet marjoram choped very small and a littell beefe-suet choped very small then put it to ye bread with nutmegg, sugar and a littell salt then put it into a bag. Boyle it for ye space of an hower. If you will make sauce to it you must take butter, sugar and rosewater."

From a 17th century manuscript Receipt Book.

Cakes & Puddings

Bath Buns
Sally Lunn Cakes
Testing a Stone Oven
Somerset Apple Cheese Pancakes
Avalon Pudding
Yeovil Baked Pears
Bath Ground Rice Pudding

BATH BUNS

Since Roman times the beautiful city of Bath or Aquae Sulis has been famous for its medicinal waters, and, since the 18th century, for its architectural elegance. Visitors can listen to the Pump Room orchestra while sampling the spa waters or enjoying a cup of tea and a Bath Bun.

Ingredients
Makes about 12

3/4oz (15g) yeast, creamed with 1 teaspoon sugar
1/2 pint (275ml) warm milk
1lb (450g) flour
4oz (110g) butter
4oz (110g) caster sugar
3 small eggs, beaten
3 heaped tablespoons chopped mixed peel
2oz (50g) coarse sugar for topping
Pinch of salt

Method
Add the creamed yeast to the warm milk and pour into the warmed flour and salt. Knead lightly. Cream the butter and sugar, add the eggs and mix into the dough together with the peel, reserving a little peel for decoration. Cover and leave to rise in a warm place for 40 minutes. Shape into buns, place on a greased baking sheet, brush with a little egg or milk, sprinkle with coarse sugar and decorate with a piece of chopped peel. Bake in a preheated oven at 180°C (350°F) gas mark 4 for about 30 minutes.

SALLY LUNN CAKES

These hot, golden cakes, were baked and sold in the streets of Bath in the eighteenth century by Sally Lunn, whose house in Old Lilliput Alley is one of the few medieval buildings remaining in Bath.

Ingredients
Makes about 8 cakes

1 ½lb (700g) plain flour with pinch of salt
1oz (25g) yeast creamed with
2 tablespoons sugar
4oz (110g) butter
1 pint (570ml) lukewarm milk
3 eggs

Method
Beat the yeast to a cream with the sugar. Soften the butter in the lukewarm milk and mix with the yeast. Put the flour and salt in a bowl and gradually stir in the yeast mixture. Add two well beaten eggs. Mix and knead lightly until a stiff dough is formed. Cover with a cloth and leave to rise in a warm place for about 2 hours, then knead again until smooth. Shape into about 8 cakes and place on a greased baking tray. Brush the tops with the yolk of the remaining egg. Bake in a hot oven at 200°C (400°F) gas mark 6 for about 20 minutes, or until firm when pressed. The cakes should be eaten just warm and may be filled with whipped cream mixed with stiffly beaten egg white.

TESTING A STONE OVEN

The stone oven was the old cottage baking oven. It was built to one side of an open fire and lined with bricks.

"Put in your sticks and set them alight, and when they are all burnt up the oven will be hot through. Draw out all of the fire from the oven, take a bit of stick and strike the floor of the oven with it. If sparks fly then you know it's just the right heat for baking bread or cake."

Traditional

SOMERSET APPLE CHEESE PANCAKES

Pancakes have been around since the Middle Ages, when they accompanied many different dishes. English pancakes are distinguished by being rolled up and the fillings, savoury or sweet, are many and varied. Apart from Cheddar cheese, Somerset produces a soft cream cheese - delicious with apple in a pancake.

Ingredients
Serves 8

Batter:
4oz (110g) flour
1 egg
1/2 pint (275ml) milk
Pinch of salt

Filling:
8oz (225g) soft cheese
1 dessert apple
4oz (110g) raisins
Zest of lemon
Caster sugar for dredging

Method

Beat together the batter ingredients, and make 8 pancakes. Keep pancakes warm between two plates over a pan of simmering water. Peel, core and finely chop or grate the apple and mix with the cheese, raisins and lemon juice. Divide the filling between the pancakes, roll up and dredge with caster sugar and serve, if desired, with fresh soured cream.

AVALON PUDDING

The name Avalon comes from the Celtic word for 'Island of apples.' Legend has it that King Arthur was carried here to die. Today this area is known as Glastonbury Tor.

Ingredients
Serves 4

8oz (225g) cooking apples
6oz (175g) white breadcrumbs
4oz (110g) suet
2oz (50g) flour
2oz (50g) caster sugar
3 eggs
1/4 teaspoon nutmeg
Grated rind of 1 lemon

Method

Mix together the breadcrumbs, flour, sugar and suet. Peel, core and chop the apples and add to the breadcrumb mixture, together with the lemon rind and nutmeg. Add the eggs, lightly beaten, and mix well. Turn the mixture into a well greased pudding basin, cover securely with foil, pleated in the centre to allow for expansion, and steam or boil for 2½-3 hours. Turn the pudding out onto a warmed dish and serve with fresh cream or custard.

YEOVIL BAKED PEARS

Pears were common in many country gardens, particularly the hard cooking pears, and many puddings and preserves were created to make best use of them. These fruits were traditionally cooked in a slow oven with cider or wine to flavour and soften them.

Ingredients
Serves 4

4 firm pears, cored, skinned and halved
2oz (50g) sultanas
1/4 pint (150ml) medium cider
1/2oz (10g) butter
1/2-1oz (10-25g) demerara sugar

Method
Put the sultanas and cider in a small saucepan and bring to the boil. Remove from the heat and allow to stand for about 15 minutes. Place the prepared pears in a shallow ovenproof dish and pour the cider and sultanas over them. Dot with butter and sprinkle with sugar, then cover and cook in a preheated oven at 180°C (350°F) gas mark 4 for about 35 minutes, or until the pears are tender. Serve with double or clotted cream.

BATH GROUND RICE PUDDING

Ingredients
Serves 4

8oz (225g) shortcrust pastry
1/2 pint (275ml) cream
1/2 pint (275ml) milk
2oz (50g) ground rice
2 eggs
1oz (25g) caster sugar
1oz (25g) butter cut into small pieces
1 teaspoon sherry or vanilla essence
Nutmeg

Method

Roll out the pastry to line an 8" (20cm) greased flan tin and bake blind in a preheated oven at 200°C (400°F) gas mark 6. Warm the cream and milk in a saucepan, sprinkle in the ground rice, stirring continuously. Add the sugar and, still stirring, bring to simmering point. Simmer over gentle heat for 5 minutes, until thickened. Then remove from the heat and allow to cool a little. Beat the eggs then add to the mixture together with the butter and sherry (or essence). Fill baked pastry case with mixture. Bake for 30 minutes at 160°C (325°F) gas mark 3. Before serving, sprinkle with nutmeg.

Drinks

Mulled Cider Cup
Wassail Punch
Mulled Cider and Red Wine Punch

MULLED CIDER CUP

Cider apple trees are often old and gnarled, planted long ago in any bit of land the farmer could spare. At harvest time cider was part of a labourer's wages. Some traditional names of apples used to make cider, or 'scrumpy' were: Slap ma Girdle, Fox Whelp, Loyal Drain, Cap of Liberty, Bloody Butcher and Porter's Perfection. Scrumping, or raiding apple orchards, is a favourite pastime of children in the West Country, great fun, unless the farmer catches you!

Ingredients
Serves 12

3 bottles dry cider
2 oranges
2 bananas
4 tablespoons brown sugar
4 cloves
1/4 teaspoon grated nutmeg
1/4 teaspoon grated cinnamon

Method

Spike the oranges with the cloves and cut into slices. Heat the cider slowly in a saucepan with the sugar, sliced oranges and spices until almost boiling. Add the thinly sliced bananas and serve at once.

WASSAIL PUNCH

Wassailing apple trees is an ancient custom thought to encourage a better harvest. The word 'wassail' comes from the Anglo Saxon greeting 'was hail' meaning 'Good health'. On Twelfth Night apple trees are wassailed by having scrumpy (rough cider) poured over their roots.

"Wassaile the trees, that they might beare
You many a plum and many a peare;
For more or less fruits they will bring
As you do give them wassailing."

Robert Herrick, 1648

Ingredients
Serves 8

3 small red apples
2 pints (1.1litres) brown ale
1/2 pint (275ml) dry sherry or dry white wine
3oz (75g) brown sugar
Strip of lemon peel
1/4 teaspoon ground cinnamon
1/4 teaspoon ground ginger
1/4 teaspoon grated nutmeg

Method
Cut through the skin round the centre of the apples and place in a 1¾ pint (1 litre) flameproof casserole. Add the brown sugar and 4 tablespoons of ale. Cover and bake in a preheated oven at 180°C (350°F) gas mark 4 for 20-30 minutes, or until the apples are tender. Remove the apples and put to one side. Pour the rest of the ale and sherry or wine into the casserole, add the spices and lemon peel and simmer over a low heat for about 5 minutes. Add the apples and serve hot.

MULLED CIDER AND RED WINE PUNCH

Try this cider and red wine punch on a cold and rainy winter evening.

Ingredients
Makes enough for 24 wine glasses

4 cooking apples
4 cloves
2 pints (1.1litres) dry cider
2 bottles red wine
2 cinnamon sticks
4oz (110g) granulated sugar
4 dessert apples
2 lemons

Method
Stick a clove into each of the cooking apples, place on a tray and bake in a preheated oven at 180°C (350°F) gas mark 4 for 30 minutes. Meanwhile, bring the cider to the boil in a saucepan, add the sugar and simmer until the sugar is dissolved. Add the wine, cinnamon sticks and baked apples. Heat gently but do not boil again. Strain the liquid. Cut the dessert apples and lemons into slices and add to the punch. Serve hot.

WEST
COUNTRY
LARDER

Traditional Recipes from

DORSET

Compiled by Alison Ainsworth and Yvonne Dawe

Peninsula
Press

Published by Peninsula Press
P.O. Box 31
Newton Abbot
Devon TQ12 5XH

Editorial, Design and Production:
A&B Creative Services
Kingskerswell
Devon TQ12 5EZ
Tel: 0803 873599

Sales and Distribution:
Town & Country Books
Kingskerswell
Devon TQ12 5AZ
Tel: 0803 875875

Printed in England by Penwell Ltd, Callington, Cornwall.

The publishers would like to thank the many people of Dorset who
have contributed to this book.

ISBN 1 872640 03 6

WEST COUNTRY LARDER
· DORSET ·

∽ Contents ∾

INTRODUCTION

With its rolling hills and downs and a coastline boasting the most varied geology in Europe, Dorset is one of the most beautiful counties in Britain. Farming has always been important here, not only for dairy products such as the famous Blue Vinney cheese - traditionally served with crisp rolls called Dorset Knobs - but also for sheep, cattle and a wide variety of vegetables and fruit. The Dorset Horn, a white faced sheep prized for its tender meat, frequently breeds out of season, and Lamb's Tail Pie was once a favourite dish.

Rabbit was also popular, with rabbit farming widely practised to ensure a regular supply. Tipsy Rabbit, a warming casserole of rabbit pieces simmered slowly in light ale with bacon and apples, is just as delicious as other, more expensive cuts of meat.

In common with the rest of the West Country, Dorset produces good crops of apples, with names such as Bloody Butcher, Sheep's Nose and Iron Apple, and the many cooking varieties are used to make a variety of dishes, including Blackberry and Apple Meringue Pie, a delightful concoction of fragrant fruit topped with frothy meringue.

Cider has always been a popular drink here, and another local drink, Dorset Ale, was mentioned by Thomas Hardy, the famous novelist and poet, whose stories about country life in nineteenth century 'Wessex' have absorbed generations of readers.

Soups

Savoy Cream Soup
Easy Peasy Soup
Cabbage Soup

SAVOY CREAM SOUP

Pumpkins deserve a better fate than being made into lanterns on All Hallows night, and this delicious soup will ward off any winter chills.

Ingredients
Serves **4**

1lb (450g) pumpkin
2 medium leeks
2 medium potatoes
1/2 pint (275ml) milk
1/2 pint (275ml) water
2oz (50g) butter, plus a knob to finish
Salt and pepper
Chopped parsley to garnish

Method

Peel pumpkin and potatoes and cut into small cubes. Wash and slice leeks. Melt the butter in a large saucepan, add the vegetables and cook over a gentle heat for about five minutes. Add the milk and water and season to taste. Simmer, covered, for 30 minutes, then mash with a fork or put through a blender.

Add the knob of butter just before serving. Sprinkle with parsley and serve piping hot.

EASY PEASY SOUP

London is not alone in having thick fogs, or pea soupers. The undulating hills of Dorset have their fair share of mists, when the ghosts of ancient Romans can be imagined around every corner!

Ingredients
Serves 6

4oz (110g) diced bacon
4oz (110g) diced carrots
4oz (110g) diced celery
4oz (110g) chopped onions
1oz (25g) butter
1lb (450g) split dried peas, soaked
overnight in cold water
4 pints (just over 2 litres) ham stock
Sprig of mint
Salt and pepper

Method
Melt the butter in a large saucepan and fry the bacon over a gentle heat for about five minutes. Add the carrots, celery and onions and cook for a further five minutes, or until the onions become transparent. Rinse the soaked peas well under running water, then add to the pan, together with the stock and the sprig of mint. Bring to a gentle simmer and cook for about 2½ hours. Skim off any froth that appears.

Rub the mixture through a sieve, or liquidise in a blender. Return to the pan and heat thoroughly. Season with salt and pepper. To turn this soup into a substantial meal, add good quality frankfurter sausages cut into bite-sized pieces.

CABBAGE SOUP

Dorset has the distinction of being the first place in England to grow cultivated cabbage.

"Take a large cabbage, chopped, one large onion, sliced, four sticks of celery, washed and sliced, and a crushed clove of garlic. Put these in a large saucepan together with some streaky bacon, ham, and half a pound of dried peas which have been soaked overnight. Add two pints of boiling water and simmer for four hours. Season with salt and pepper and add a dash of vinegar just before serving."

Traditional

Meat & Fish

Lyme Bay Haddock Casserole

Red Mullet

Magog Mackerel

Long Puddle Lamb

Lamb's Tail Pie

Tipsy Rabbit

Puddle Bacon Cake

Rooky Pie

Dorset Casserole with Dumplings

Dorset Sausage

Dorset Jugged Steak

To Dress Beef Steaks

To Draw Gravey

Sorrel Purée

LYME BAY HADDOCK CASSEROLE

Good fresh fish is readily available in Dorset, and this recipe is equally good using either haddock or cod.

Ingredients
Serves 2-3

1lb (450g) haddock or cod fillet
8oz (225g) tomatoes, peeled and sliced
2oz (50g) button mushrooms, sliced
1 medium onion, chopped
1 tablespoon chopped parsley
1/4 pint (150ml) cider
2 tablespoons fresh white breadcrumbs
2oz (50g) grated Cheddar cheese
Salt and freshly ground black pepper

Method

Skin the fish and cut into cubes. Put the fish in a casserole, cover with the tomatoes, mushrooms and onion, then sprinkle with the parsley and seasonings. Pour over the cider, cover and bake at 180°C (350°F) gas mark 4, for 20-25 minutes or until the fish is cooked. Mix together the breadcrumbs and cheese, and sprinkle on top of the fish. Place under a hot grill until the cheese and breadcrumbs are golden brown.

RED MULLET

Sometimes called the 'woodcock of the sea', because like the game bird of that name it is better cooked with its liver intact.

Ingredients
Serves 2

2 red mullet
2oz (50g) breadcrumbs
2oz (50g) melted butter
1 teaspoon chopped fennel
2 teaspoons chopped parsley
Juice of half a lemon
Salt and pepper

Method
Cut off head, tail and fins or ask your fishmonger to do it for you. Score the fish on both sides. Butter a shallow ovenproof dish, place the fish in it, then sprinkle with salt, pepper, parsley, fennel and lemon juice. Pour over the melted butter, cover with foil and bake at 180°C (350°F) gas mark 4 for 20 minutes, basting several times during cooking.
Serve with a green salad and wholemeal bread.

MAGOG MACKEREL

A wide variety of fish is to be found in the sea off the Dorset coast, including bass, black bream, cod, dab, flounder, garfish, mullet, plaice, sole, whiting and of course mackerel, which is probably the most prolific, and which needs only simple cooking.

Ingredients
Serves 4

4 medium mackerel
8oz (225g) gooseberries
2oz (50g) butter
3 tablespoons breadcrumbs
Salt and black pepper

Method
Top, tail and clean the mackerel, and do the same with the gooseberries. Heat and soften the gooseberries in the butter over a low heat until slightly mushy. Allow to cool slightly, then add salt, pepper and breadcrumbs to make a manageable stuffing.

Open the mackerel, lay it skin side up and press firmly with your thumbs down the back to loosen the bone. Turn the fish over and lift the backbone away from the flesh. Divide the stuffing into four and fill each fish. Close the fish and lay in a well buttered ovenproof dish. Cover with foil and bake at 180°C (350°F) gas mark 4 for 30 minutes. Serve with crusty bread, Dorset butter and a green salad.

LONG PUDDLE LAMB

The Dorset Horn is a white faced sheep which is valued worldwide, both for its tender meat and its medium length wool. Some of the ewes breed out of season and the lambs grow rapidly in the lush green Dorset meadows.

Ingredients
Serves 4-6

1 ½lb (700g) leg or shoulder of lamb, boned
2 ½oz (60g) butter
2 small onions
1 clove garlic
2 tablespoons Worcestershire sauce
2 tablespoons chopped parsley
1/4 pint (150ml) stock
1/4 pint (150ml) cider
Flour, salt and pepper

Method
Cut the meat into cubes and coat with seasoned flour. Peel and chop the onion and crush the garlic. Heat the butter in a large, heavy-based saucepan and brown the meat in it. Transfer the meat to a casserole together with the onion, garlic and parsley. Add the stock and cider to the juices in the saucepan and stir until boiling. Now add the Worcestershire sauce and seasoning and simmer for 5 minutes. Pour over the meat, cover and cook in a preheated oven at 190°C (375°F) gas mark 5 for an hour or until tender.
Serve with plain boiled potatoes and vegetables. This dish can be cooked in advance as it reheats very well.

LAMB'S TAIL PIE

No Dorset feast would have been complete without this tasty pie.

"Take lambs' tails from Dorset Horns and put them in a pie dish with some bacon, hard boiled eggs, fresh herbs, lemon peel and seasoning. Pour over some stock and cover with pastry."

Traditional

TIPSY RABBIT

Rabbit was once the staple diet of country folk, and in addition to the wild variety, rabbit farming was also widely practised, hence the proliferation of 'Warren Inns' throughout the county.

Ingredients
Serves 4

1 ½lb (700g) rabbit pieces
6oz (175g) bacon, chopped
2 medium onions, peeled and chopped
1 cooking apple, cored and sliced
8 stoned prunes
1 medium carrot, chopped
1 celery stalk, chopped
1/2 pint (275ml) light beer
Salt and pepper
Nutmeg

Method

Fry the bacon until the fat runs. Transfer to casserole and fry the rabbit pieces in the bacon fat until lightly browned on all sides. Place on top of the bacon. Now fry onions and apple until golden but not browned. Add to casserole, together with the prunes, carrot, celery and beer. Season with salt, pepper and freshly grated nutmeg.

Cover and cook in a preheated oven at 170°C (325°F) gas mark 3 for 1 ½ - 2 hours or until the meat is tender. Serve with parsley potatoes and minty peas.

PUDDLE BACON CAKE

This was originally known as 'Piddle Bacon Cake', after the River Piddle, but the name was changed to Puddle, to spare the blushes of Victorian cooks!

Ingredients
Serves 4

1 ½lb (700g) minced lean bacon
1 ½oz (40g) butter
2 ½oz (60g) soft brown sugar
1 tablespoon minced onion
2 large pineapple rings
2 slightly beaten eggs
2oz (50g) stale breadcrumbs
4 Maraschino cherries
10 whole cloves
1/2 teaspoon mustard powder
1/4 teaspoon black pepper

Method

Melt the butter and dissolve the sugar in it. Use this mixture to cover the base of a round 7" (18cm) cake tin. Cut the pineapple rings into wedges and place in a decorative pattern over the base of the cake tin. Mix the remaining ingredients until thoroughly blended, spread over pineapple base, press down firmly, stud with cloves and bake in a moderate oven 180°C (350°F) gas mark 4 for 1 hour.

Remove cloves and turn 'cake' onto a large heated platter and decorate the top with cherries. Surround the base of the platter with watercress.

ROOKY PIE

The 'good olde days' were not so good for villagers who had to exist on very low wages, or in some cases no wages at all. Food was obtained from whatever sources were available.

"Take four good rooks, pluck them, chop off the heads and feet, and cut into four pieces each. Put in a large pie dish with some veal, bacon and stock, and cover with a pastry lid. Bake for one hour. Serve with caution."

Traditional

DORSET CASSEROLE WITH DUMPLINGS

Ingredients
Serves 4

1lb (450g) lean braising steak
1 medium onion, chopped
2oz (50g) mushrooms, sliced
8oz (225g) carrots, diced

8oz (225g) turnips, diced
1 tablespoon cooking oil
1 tablespoon plain flour
1/2 pint (275ml) good quality beef stock
1/4 pint (150ml) cider
Salt and pepper

Method

Heat the oil in a flameproof casserole or heavy frying pan. Cut the meat into 2" (5cm) cubes and brown thoroughly in the oil. Remove from the pan, using a slotted spoon. Add the vegetables to the pan and cook over a low heat for 5-7 minutes, stirring occasionally. Stir in the flour and continue cooking gently, stirring constantly, for two minutes. Remove from the heat and gradually whisk in the cider and stock. Return pan to the heat and bring to the boil, stirring constantly. Add the meat to the casserole and season to taste. Cover and cook in a preheated oven at 180°C (350°F) gas mark 4, for 2 hours or until the meat is tender.

Ingredients for the dumplings

4oz (110g) self raising flour
2oz (50g) beef or vegetable suet
1 tablespoonful chopped parsley
Milk to mix
Salt and pepper

Method

Mix together the flour, suet, parsley, salt and pepper and stir in enough milk to make a firm dough. Shape into 12 even-sized balls with floured hands. Approximately 25 minutes before the end of the cooking time remove the casserole from the oven, stir well and adjust the seasoning. Place the dumplings on top of the meat, and return the casserole to the oven, uncovered, for the remainder of the cooking time.

DORSET SAUSAGE

This isn't a sausage at all, but a coarse terrine, or meat loaf. It makes an ideal dish for a picnic or cold supper and is best made the day before it is eaten.

Ingredients
Serves 8

1lb (450g) minced beef
1lb (450g) minced ham or bacon
6oz (175g) fresh breadcrumbs
2 tablespoons chopped parsley
2 eggs
2 teaspoons Worcestershire sauce
1/2teaspoon ground mace
1/2 nutmeg, grated
Salt and pepper

Method
Mix the beef and ham or bacon in a bowl together with the breadcrumbs. Beat the eggs then stir into the meat mixture and add the spices and seasoning. Make sure everything is well blended then grease a large oblong cake tin and spoon the mixture into it. Cover the top with foil and place the tin in a roasting tin containing 1-2" (2-5cm) warm water. Bake in a preheated oven at 170°C (325°F) gas mark 3 for 1½ hours.

Remove from oven, then leave overnight to get completely cold. Turn out of the tin and decorate with sliced pickled gherkins. Cut into thick slices and serve with toast and salad.

DORSET JUGGED STEAK

A rich beef casserole which has the 'jugged' flavour associated with hare. The sausagemeat balls are also excellent with game or as a stuffing for chicken or turkey. Very filling!

Ingredients
Serves 4-6

2lb (900g) shin of beef
1 large onion
1/4 pint (150ml) stock
2 tablespoons port or red wine (optional)
2 teaspoons redcurrant jelly
4 cloves
1 teaspoon dried mixed herbs
Flour, salt and pepper
Beef dripping or oil

Ingredients for the meat balls

8oz (225g) sausagemeat
1 cup breadcrumbs
1 egg
Salt and pepper

Method
Cut the beef into cubes, roll in seasoned flour and fry lightly on both sides in dripping or oil. Transfer to a large ovenproof casserole and add the chopped onion, stock and red wine if used. Top up with water, if necessary, to just cover. Add cloves, mixed herbs and seasoning, stir well and cover. Cook in a preheated oven at 150°C (300°F) gas mark 2 for about 2 hours, checking occasionally to see that the liquid has not run dry. Top up with stock or water as required.

Method for the meat balls

Mix together the sausagemeat, breadcrumbs and beaten egg, and season with salt and pepper. With floured hands, divide the mixture into a number of walnut-sized balls. Poach in boiling water for 5-10 minutes, removing any scum as it forms. Drain and set aside.

When the casserole is thoroughly cooked, stir in the redcurrant jelly and add the sausagemeat balls. Return the casserole, uncovered, to the oven for a further 10 minutes.
Serve with potatoes baked in their jackets and carrots.

TO DRESS BEEF STAKES

"Take goode buttock beef & cut it in thin slices, & chop it as you doe for Scotch Scollops wash them all over with Eggs on both sides & strew them over pretty thick with Crumbs of bread mixt with sweet herbs, a little pepper & salt, fry them with very little liquor for the sauce take a little Gravy, Anchovy, & butter, & Lemon if you please . . ."

From a 17th century Receipt Book.

TO DRAW GRAVEY

"Take some slices of buttock Beife hack it with ye back of a Knife put it into a frying pan fry them with a little fresh butter just enough to brown then put in a pint of water an oynion a bunch of sweet hearbs a little whole pepper & 2 or 3 anchovies so let it stew leisurely over ye fire till half ye licquor is wasted then squeese out the juce of ye meat between 2 trenchers and keep it for your use . . ."

From a 17th century Receipt Book.

SORREL PURÉE

"Sorrel sharpens the appetite assuages heat, cools the liver, and strengthens the heart . . ."

John Evelyn 1699

In addition to being served as a vegetable or in soups sorrel was also used as a purgative and as a cure for toothache. Farm workers chewed its leaves to quench their thirst.

French sorrel has tender young leaves with a lemony flavour that makes a delicious accompaniment for chicken, ham, white fish or eggs.

Ingredients
Serves 4

2lb (900g) sorrel
2 eggs
1/4 pint (150ml) double cream
1 ½oz (40g) butter
1/4 teaspoon grated nutmeg
Salt and pepper

Method
Wash and chop the sorrel. Melt the butter in a large heavy based pan, and cook the sorrel, covered, for about 5 minutes until tender. Remove the lid and add the cream and the eggs, beaten. Season with salt and pepper and simmer gently, uncovered, stirring frequently, until the mixture thickens. Do not allow to come to the boil. Serve sprinkled with nutmeg.

Cakes & Puddings

Sweetheart Cake

Blackmore Vale Cake

Blackberry and Apple Meringue Pie

Golden Cap Pudding

Apple Frumenty

Rennet

Wessex Junket

SWEETHEART CAKE

Wishing wells are frequently to be found in Dorset, and many a hopeful lad or lass sat by one and recited this sweet little couplet on Midsummer's Eve.

*"Hoping this night
My truelove to see,
I place my shoes
In the form of a T."*

Ingredients

*2oz (50g) butter
4oz (110g) sugar
8oz (225g) plain flour
2 eggs
2oz (50g) chopped almonds
1 teaspoon baking powder
8oz (225g) sifted icing sugar
Ratafia essence
Water
Crystallised or fresh roses*

Method

Cream butter and sugar until soft, then beat in the eggs one at a time. Sieve the flour and baking powder and stir into the mixture. Add the chopped almonds. Transfer to a buttered cake tin (heart shaped if you have one) and bake in a preheated oven at 180°C (350°F) gas mark 4 for about 50 minutes. Remove from the tin after 10 minutes and allow to cool on a wire rack. When cold cover with water icing made with the icing sugar, ratafia essence and water, and decorate with crystallised or fresh roses.

BLACKMORE VALE CAKE

This cake has been eaten by the Blackmore Vale Hunt for over 100 years.

Ingredients

4oz (110g) butter
4oz (110g) caster sugar
12oz (350g) plain flour
12oz (350g) raisins
3oz (75g) chopped mixed peel
1 teaspoon bicarbonate of soda
2 teaspoons golden syrup
1/4pt (150ml) milk

Method

Cream together the butter and sugar. Heat the milk and dissolve the bicarbonate of soda and syrup in it. Add the sieved flour gradually to the butter and sugar mixture, alternately with the milk mixture, beating well. Stir in the raisins and chopped mixed peel. Transfer to a lined and greased 6" (15cm) cake tin and bake in the centre of a preheated oven at 180°C (350°F) gas mark 4 for 2½ hours.

BLACKBERRY AND APPLE MERINGUE PIE

Orchards and hedgerows flourish in Dorset and you can combine a delightful walk with gathering the ingredients for this unusual pudding.

Ingredients

8oz (225g) shortcrust pastry
3 Bramley cooking apples
8oz (225g) blackberries
4oz (110g) brown sugar
Pinch of ground cloves
2 egg whites
3 tablespoons sifted icing sugar
2-3 tablespoons water

Method

Line a pie dish with the shortcrust pastry and bake blind at the top of a preheated oven at 200°C (400°F) gas mark 6 for 10 minutes. Reset the oven to 170°C (325°F) gas mark 3. Peel, core and slice the apples and simmer gently together with the blackberries, sugar, ground cloves and the water until softened. Leave to cool for about 10 minutes, before spooning the mixture carefully onto the pastry base. Beat the egg whites until they form stiff peaks, then fold in the icing sugar and continue beating until glossy. Spoon the meringue over the pie and return to the middle of the oven for 20 minutes.

GOLDEN CAP PUDDING

If you can bear to leave the pretty highway through Chideock, take the sea road to the beach called Seatown. Here in all its glory you will see the beautiful rising cliff face known as Golden Cap.

Ingredients

6oz (175g) self-raising flour
4oz (110g) soft margarine

4oz (110g) caster sugar
2 lightly beaten eggs
2 tablespoons marmalade
Finely grated rind and juice of one large orange

Method

Spread the marmalade in the base of a buttered 2 pint (1.1 litre) pudding basin. Sift the flour into a mixing bowl and add the sugar, margarine and eggs. Beat for 2-3 minutes until the mixture is light and fluffy, add the orange juice and rind and blend thoroughly together. Spoon the mixture into the basin and cover the top with greased foil, pleated in the centre to allow the pudding to rise during steaming. Secure with string. Place in a large saucepan containing enough boiling water to reach halfway up the sides of the basin. Cover and steam for 2 hours, topping up with more water as necessary. Do not allow to boil dry. Allow to cool slightly before turning out onto a serving dish. Serve with single cream.

APPLE FRUMENTY

This is a more palatable version of the 'furmity' sold to country folk visiting the fairs that came annually to the West Country. Indeed it was 'furmity' laced with rum that led to the dreadful deed of the Mayor of Casterbridge, in Thomas Hardy's novel.

Ingredients

4 large Bramley cooking apples
4oz (110g) dark muscovado sugar
1/4 pint (150ml) cider
1/4 pint (150ml) water
1/2 teaspoon powdered cinnamon
Toasted almonds for topping

Method

Peel, core and slice the apples and place in a saucepan together with the sugar, cinnamon, cider and water. Cook until soft and mushy. Turn into a bowl, sprinkle toasted almonds on top, and serve with a thin pouring custard or single cream.

RENNET

"Let the calf suck as much as he will, just before he is killed. Take the milk bag out of the calf and let it lie 12 hours covered with stinging nettles till it is red. Then take out your curd and wash the bag clean and salt it inside and out. Let it lie in salt for 24 hours, then wash your curd in new milk and clean it and put it back in the bag with 3 or 4 streakings [the last milk from the cow], *a beaten egg, 10 cloves, a blade of mace, and skewer the bag shut and hang in a pot.*

In another pot put 1/2 pint of salted water, 5 tops of the reddish blackthorn, the same of burnet, 3 of sweet marjoram and boil altogether, let it cool, then put some of this flavoured water into the bag with the egg and milk and let the bag soak in the rest of it. This in which the bag lies (and into which the heavier liquid from inside the bag exudes) is the rennet, and it is so strong that the bag can be refilled and left to exude more than 6 or 7 times before the curdling action of the stomach juice is exhausted."

From a 16th century recipe.

WESSEX JUNKET

Fortunately we can now buy rennet in a bottle, and the simple dish of junket was frequently used as a test of skill at agricultural shows. The ideal temperature for the milk was as it came straight from the cow, a practice that would be greatly frowned upon nowadays.

Ingredients

1/2 pint (275ml) milk
1/2 pint (275ml) Dorset cream
1 ½oz (40g) caster sugar
1 teaspoon rennet
Nutmeg

Method

Mix the milk and cream together in a saucepan and sprinkle in the sugar. Warm this slowly until the sugar has dissolved and the milk is no more than blood heat. Stir in the rennet, pour immediately into a large shallow serving dish, and leave in a cool place to set. Do not refrigerate. Before serving, grate nutmeg evenly over the surface.

Drinks

Dorset Claret Cup
Almond Shrub
Mulled Ale
Ginger Beer

DORSET CLARET CUP

Ingredients

1 bottle light claret
1 bottle soda water
1 wine glass pounded sugar
1 large glass sherry
1 small glass curacao
The thinly pared rind of a lemon
Slices of cucumber
Sprigs of mint or borage

Method

Simply combine the first six ingredients in a glass punchbowl and garnish with slices of cucumber and sprigs of mint or borage. Chill before serving.

ALMOND SHRUB

"Take 3 gallons of rum or brandy, 3 quarts of orange juice, the peel of 3 lemons, 3lb of loaf sugar, then 4oz of bitter almonds, blanch and beat them fine, mix them all well together, let it stand an hour to curdle, run it through a flannel bag several times till it is clear, then bottle for use."

Traditional recipe

MULLED ALE

Ingredients

3 eggs
1 pint (570ml) ale
4oz (110g) caster sugar
2 pints (1.1 litre) milk
1/4 nutmeg, grated

Method

Bring the ale to the boil in a saucepan. Remove from the heat, beat the eggs well and stir into the milk. Add the ale, sugar and nutmeg and heat slowly, stirring constantly until the mixture thickens. Do not allow to boil. Pour into a jug and stir for 2 minutes.

GINGER BEER

This was a popular drink amongst country folk, especially farm workers at harvest time.

Ingredients
Makes one gallon (4.5 litres)

1oz (25g) root beer
1lb (450g) sugar
1 large lemon
1oz (25g) cream of tartar
1oz (25g) fresh yeast
8 pints (4.5 litres) boiling water

Method
Bruise the ginger by wrapping it in a cloth and hitting it with a steak tenderiser or hammer. This helps to release the flavour.

Peel the rind thinly from the lemon, then squeeze out the juice. Put the ginger, sugar, lemon rind and cream of tartar into a two gallon (9 litre) plastic bucket, then add the boiling water and the lemon juice. Stir well and leave to cool to 21°C (70°F). Cream the yeast to a smooth paste with a little warm water and stir it into the mixture. Cover the bucket with a clean cloth and secure with string or rubber bands. Leave in a warm place for 24 hours to ferment.

Skim off the froth and, being careful not to disturb the sediment, ladle the beer into clean, strong bottles, with the aid of a funnel if necessary. Cork the bottles, securing the corks with string or fine wire. Store the bottles in a cool place and keep an eye on them. The ginger beer should be ready to drink in 3-4 days, but the wires or string may need to be adjusted as the beer continues to ferment and pressure builds up.